BEAT THE BINGE

CONTROL YOUR IMPULSIVE OVEREATING WORKBOOK

BY DR. YULIYA RICHARD, PSYD CLINICAL AND HEALTH PSYCHOLOGY

ILLUSTRATIONS BY OVIDIU AMBROZIE BORTĂ

www.impulsivity.com.au

Copyright 2022-All rights reserved for Impulsivity.com.au

The content contained within this workbook is licensed for your personal use only. This workbook may not be reproduced, duplicated or transmitted without direct written permission from the author or the publisher.

Under no circumstances will any blame or legal responsibility be held against the publisher, or author, for any damages, reparation, or monetary loss due to the information contained within this book, either directly or indirectly.

No part of this book may be used or reproduced by any means, graphic, electronic, or mechanical, including photocopying, recording, taping or by any information storage retrieval system without the written permission of the publisher except in the case of brief quotations embodied in critical articles and reviews.

Legal Notice:

This workbook is copyright protected. It is only for personal use. You cannot amend, distribute, sell, use, quote or paraphrase any part, of the content within this book, without the consent of the author or publisher.

Disclaimer Notice:

Please note the information contained within this document is for educational and entertainment purposes only. All effort has been executed to present accurate, up to date, reliable, complete information. No warranties of any kind are declared or implied. Readers acknowledge that the author is not engaged in the rendering of legal, financial, medical or professional advice. The content within this book has been derived from various sources. Please consult a licensed professional before attempting any techniques outlined in this book.

By reading this document, the reader agrees that under no circumstances is the author responsible for any lossess, direct or indirect, that are incurred as a result of the use of the information contained within this document, including, but not limited to errors, omissions, or inaccuracies.

Acknowledgements

I would like to thank a few of the people who made this book possible, including Caroline Risby, Hailey Shafir, LPCS, LCAS, CCS-I, and Dr. Sirous Mobini.

The Impulsivity Online Project
Presents

Table of Contents

Introduction	VI
Part 1 - WHAT Happened To Us?	1
A Common Problem	2
Understanding Binge Eating	2
The Role of Impulsivity	5
Defining Binge Eating	7
AM I IMPULSIVE?	10
IMPULSIVITY TRACKER	11
END OF WEEK REFLECTION	12
FALSE ALARMS	14
REWIRING THE ALARM SYSTEM	15
Binge Eating Disorder or an Impulsive Binge Eating Problem?	16
Part 2 - WHY Binge Eating Occurs & What Causes It	19
5 Predispositions of Impulsivity	20
What is Dopamine	25
MY MOTIVATION TO CHANGE	28
CHANGE BELIEFS	29
FINDING YOUR PATTERNS	31
RETHINKING NEGATIVE IMPACTS	35
Pain & Pleasure Principle	36
Emotional Vs Physical Hunger	36
I'M NOT HUNGRY, I'M...	38
DAILY PROGRESS CHECKLIST	39
EXPECTATION VS. REALITY	41
Stress	43
Emotions	45
EMOTIONAL RESPONSES	48
EMOTIONAL CARE-GIVING	49
TO DO OR NOT TO DO...	52
MODERATE EATING	54
IDENTIFYING AND DEALING WITH TRIGGERS	55
IDENTIFYING YOUR TRIGGERS FOR UNHELPFUL IMPULSE BEHAVIOUR	56
Triggers	57
PLANNING AHEAD	59
FOOD DIARY	60
PERSONAL VALUES	65
Part 3 - HOW to Overcome Impulsive Overeating	68
Strategies & Tips for Addressing Overeating	69

Cognitive Behavioural Therapy	78
Cognitive Distortion Types	79
IDENTIFYING MY NEGATIVE COGNITIVE DISTORTIONS	94
DISPUTING MY IMPULSIVE THOUGHTS	96
Develop & Protect your New Mindset	99
Self-Care and Self-Compassion	101
SELF-CRITICISM VS SELF-COMPASSION	104
SELF COMPASSION LETTER	105
Mindfulness	106
MINDFULNESS PRACTICE LOG	111
Nutrition Chapter	112
The Basics of Nutrition	112
Calculating How Many Calories You Need	113
Nutrients	114
5 Practical Nutrition Strategies That You Can Try Today	116
Mindfulness vs Intuitive Eating	118
ASK MY FUTURE SELF	121
STAYING ON TRACK	122
MY TOOLBOX	124
Conclusion	125
Part 4 - Worksheets, Templates & Practical Activities	127
IMPULSE LOG	128
MODERATE EATING	129
MEASURING PROGRESS	130
ENABLERS OR TRUE SUPPORTERS? CHOOSING THE RIGHT FRIENDS	131
ADVANTAGES AND DISADVANTAGES OF IMPULSE BEHAVIOUR (UNHELPFUL IMPULSIVE BEHAVIOUR)	132
IDENTIFYING MY NEGATIVE THOUGHTS & COGNITIVE DISTORTIONS	133
LIFE WHEN I AM IN CONTROL	134
Notes	135
References	136
Impulsivity Courses	144
About the Author	151

Introduction

Let me start by saying this guide is not about shaming, applying pressure, or persuading you to lose weight. It's about helping you feel in control of your eating habits and having more control over impulsive overeating.

This book is for you if:

- you feel you are not in control of your eating habits
- you're dealing with negative consequences of this loss of control, such as putting on weight or becoming a closet overeater
- you are powerless when urges arise and most of the time end up giving in to them.

Acceptance, compassion and creating a healthy and sustainable lifestyle lies at the core of this guide. All body shapes are beautiful. Whatever your shape or size, when you have control over your eating behaviours, you can feel proud of yourself and feel in control of your life. It's time to put yourself first and change your relationship with food so you enjoy food for nourishment and enjoyment rather than as a substitute for nurture and care.

I want to help you:

- let go of maladaptive coping strategies for stress
- learn to regulate your emotions well
- correct your unhelpful thinking patterns
- practice mindfulness to better connect with yourself
- change your attitude towards yourself
- improve your self-care
- surround yourself with positive people.

> **"Control your own destiny or someone else will."**
> **~ Jack Welch ~**

Food is not your enemy. It's GOOD to enjoy food. Overconsumption is what ultimately creates problems. Instead of depriving yourself, obsessing about something, stressing about it and overeating - simply allow yourself to enjoy your favourite food. Enjoy every bite and be mindful. Control means that you can walk away after you have enjoyed a couple of bites. It means assuring yourself that if you want to eat it again - you can do it. But it's important to ensure your body is well nourished, because eating sugar alone can lead to depletion of vitamins and minerals.

This book is designed to help you beat your impulsive overeating. It'll teach you practical strategies so you can manage the thoughts and behaviours that may cause you to binge. By reading all the chapters, you'll be armed with the tools and knowledge to regain control over your life and develop a healthier relationship with food. Let's get straight into it.

You're probably reading this book because you or someone you care about has problems managing impulsive behaviours. You may have purchased it as a standalone introduction to overcoming binge eating or as part of our Beat the Binge online program. If you haven't already checked out the online course content, then we'd highly encourage you to do this now. It includes;

- video lessons that walk you step-by-step through cognitive behavioural therapy techniques and mindfulness strategies
- practical activities that allow you implement what you're learning
- printable worksheets for you to complete along the way
- library of mindfulness exercises and guided meditation recordings
- lifetime access to all of the course content and future updates.

Visit our website www.impulsivity.com.au to learn more about our comprehensive online program.

Is This Right For You?

Do you need help overcoming your binge eating?

It's a valid question and we're sure you've tried many things in the past to overcome unhealthy eating habits. Unfortunately, we know how easy it is to fall back into these habits. That's where we come in. Our courses use proven strategies for lasting change to regain control of your eating habits for good.

A quick test
Not sure whether this course applies to you? Start off by answering the below questions and if any ring true for you, then this course could be for you.
- Do you feel that you can't stop when you start eating?
- Do you obsess about food?
- Do you think about what to eat all the time?
- Do you feel sick, ashamed, or disgusted when you stop eating?
- Does eating help you to escape, to forget your worries, to comfort yourself?

Part 1 - WHAT Happened To Us?

> *"Change your thoughts and you change your world."*
> *~ Norman Vincent Peale ~*

A Common Problem

Some of the facts about obesity and being overweight are difficult to ignore. According to the World Health Organisation, 1.9 billion people over the age of 18 are overweight, and approximately 600 million are obese. Worldwide, obesity has more than doubled since 1980. Some researchers consider 70% of Millennials (people who were born between 1980 and the mid-1990s) to be struggling with their weight.

According to Australian National Health Survey results, 27.5% of Australians were obese in 2011-12. This is almost a 50% increase since 1995. In Australia, a quarter of the population is suffering from excess weight due to unhealthy lifestyle choices, particularly addictions and binge eating habits. This quarter of the population is struggling with weight management not because of an illness or circumstances that are not under their control. One of the main issues is their habitual unhealthy lifestyle choices.

Understanding Binge Eating

Some of the consequences of binge eating will be obvious and noticeable. You might look bigger, your clothes won't fit, your fitness levels change, or you get tired easily when walking upstairs or doing regular chores. We know but choose to ignore other long-term consequences, such as potential heart problems, diabetes, cardiovascular conditions, metabolic conditions and other medical issues that are often present when we struggle with our weight.

So why do we consistently ignore the negative consequences of putting on weight? Is it possible that we just focus on what is at hand? For example, right now you might choose to have a delicious cupcake and decide that tomorrow you'll focus on losing weight. But tomorrow you might forget your promise and have a Danish pastry. And so it continues, until one day you look in a mirror and it makes you feel sad. Or someone makes a comment that stings because it's true. Or you go to a shop to buy a new outfit and are told that they don't stock your size.

Is it possible that unhelpful impulsivity is at least partially to blame for this decision making? We focus on the immediate reward of a sweet, delicious pastry instead of the long-term consequences of eating Danishes for breakfast.

Your frustration at not fitting into your outfits or feeling uncomfortable in your own skin may lead you to try other ways to manage this behaviour. Maybe you spend your money on weight loss aids and programs. Sometimes supplements, diets, or boot camps. But the reality is that unless you change the way you manage your impulsive decision making around food, improve your emotional management, and create healthy and sustainable habits, none of these alternatives will work as well.

However, one of the problems that we experience when we struggle with our impulsivity is that we don't want to wait - we pay a higher price to see results now. We want it to be fixed, we react emotionally, but most likely fail to take our supplements or stop going to the gym eventually.

The cost of impulsive overeating is not only your physical changes - it has a dramatic impact on your mental and emotional health. It is hard to feel proud of yourself when you don't feel in control of your eating habits, when you feel that you can't stop until you feel full. Usually, you feel disgusted with yourself, frustrated, disappointed, or angry.

Does this sound familiar?

People who don't struggle with impulsive overeating might not understand you. You might feel alone in your struggle. You might even give up, tell yourself that this is just who you are, that it's impossible for you to change. You might even say that this is in your genes. Often, we try to hide our eating habits from others and even become closet overeaters. Impulsive overeating and putting on weight affects your self-esteem and confidence. It may lead you to feeling weak and ashamed of yourself.

This might continue until the next time you feel really unhappy with yourself and the way you look. You might receive negative news or a warning from your doctor and you might choose to react impulsively to change it. It is undeniable that with all the negative consequences for your health, excess weight eventually leads to premature death.

The bottom line is that every aspect of your life is affected when you are not in control of your eating habits: your physical health, your mental and emotional health, your self-perception and your relationships.

So, how about you? How has impulsive overeating affected your life?

What do you tell yourself when you impulsively binge eat? How do you explain it?

How would your life be different if you were in control?

The Role of Impulsivity

In order to control our eating behaviours, it's possible that we need to address the important underlying factor of impulsivity.

A recent study showed that the greater their impulsivity, the more likely overweight and obese people were to make unhealthy food choices. Interestingly, it did not have the same influence if people had leaner bodies. This might mean that you need to harness your impulsivity in order to maintain a healthy weight and establish positive eating habits.

The recent study 'Brain structure and BMI are linked' (Raji et al., 2010) showed that people who are overweight will consistently make unhealthy food choices. So, does this mean that just knowing what is good for you and how to make healthy choices is not good enough to help you be in control of your eating habits?

Why is it not enough? Why do we continue struggling with it? Why doesn't education alone work?

Some researchers believe that impulsivity plays a significant role in being overweight and obese, as well as in the development and maintenance of binge eating disorders.

"Impulsivity is perhaps the most important trait to consider for binge eating and associated eating disorders" (Leehr et al., 2015).

Another study highlights that 'it is interesting to note that individuals with high impulsivity demonstrate higher weight gain across their lifespan' (Sutin et al., 2011).

Giving in to urges can be compared with feeding a stray cat. At the beginning you want to feed the cat because it cries for food and attention. You might find that it is a nice thing to do and it feels good doing a kind deed. However, after a while the cat is encouraged to repeat its cries. And you find yourself giving in each time. Over a period of time the cat grows more confident and demands his food and attention. Other cats join him in crying for food and attention.

Now you may regret your actions, as a large number of crying cats will create noise and other problems. But you cannot ignore their cries. You may think their survival depends on you, that your actions are more important than ever.

You are trapped in a cycle of repeated problem behaviours (Chris Walsh, Mindfulness Training, 2006).

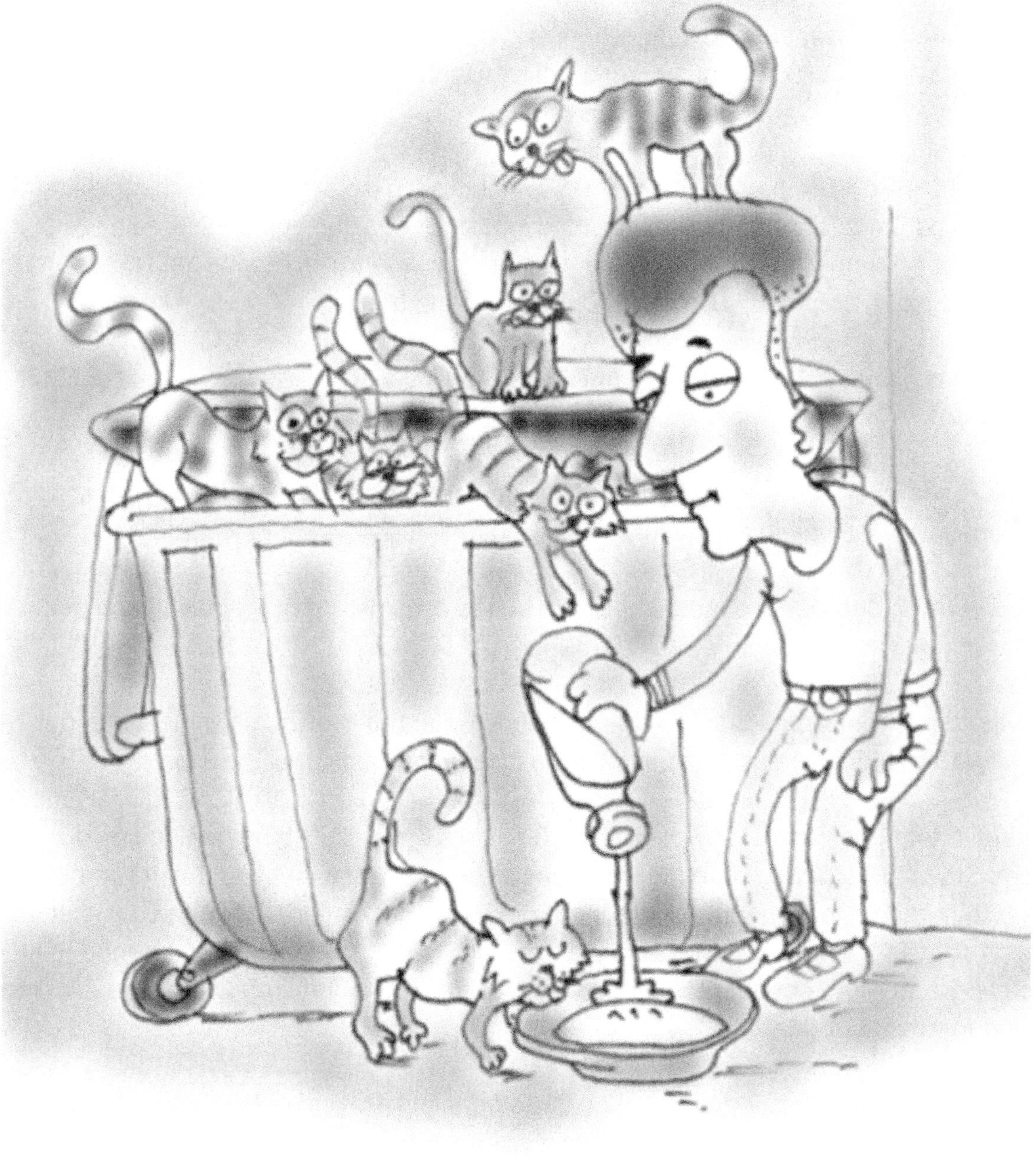

Defining Binge Eating

Impulsivity is a personality characteristic that potentially has crucial consequences for the development, maintenance, and treatment of obesity.

However, there are currently some challenges with impulsivity and our approach to overcoming it.

The first challenge is that researchers have yet to agree on a definition of impulsivity. Below, we present the five most commonly used definitions - they all sound very similar. Take a minute to look at them.

"Behaviours that are poorly conceived, premature, inappropriate and that frequently result in unwanted and deleterious outcomes."
(Chamberlain & Sahakian, 2007)

"Acting on the spur of the moment, not focusing on the task at hand, and lack of planning"
(Stratton, 2006)

Impulsivity
"Perseverance to the response that is punished and unrewarded; as well as, Preference for small immediate rewards rather than larger delayed rewards and making responses that are immature or as inability to withold a response."
(Moeller et al, 2001)

"The tendency to deliberate less than common people of equal ability before taking action."
(Dickman, 1990)

"Predisposition toward rapid, unplanned reactions to internal and external stimuli without regard to the negative consequences of these reactions to the impulsive individual or to others."
(Moeller, et al 2001)

So, what is impulsivity? Basically, it means:

- **You don't really think about what you do (you don't plan, you tend to just act)**

You might choose to pick up a Danish pastry or a muffin at a staff meeting even though you are not hungry. You might experience a trigger, like seeing your favourite food, and you eat impulsively instead of thinking about your decision to pick up this food and checking if you are actually hungry (or simply bored or frustrated).

- **You focus on immediate small rewards instead of larger later rewards despite negative consequences**

You can't wait to get what you want, such as fitness and health. You might prefer an immediate small reward such as your favourite food now rather than a larger reward later.

- **You can't resist your urges, you feel out of control**

You act as soon as you experience an urge or impulse even though it consistently leads to negative consequences. For example, you put on weight, you feel embarrassed, you fail at diets. But again and again, you choose that croissant or chips over a fit, healthy body.

As a result, day after day we engage in the same impulsive overeating, but we don't think about our actions. We don't question ourselves. So, it leads us to feel powerless, weak, and ashamed due to the lack of control over our impulsive behaviours (Grant & Kim, 2003).

When we struggle with impulsivity and impulsive behaviours, we often experience heightened anxiety, depressive moods, low self-esteem, and increased stress associated with our impulsive behaviours (Grant & Kim, 2003).

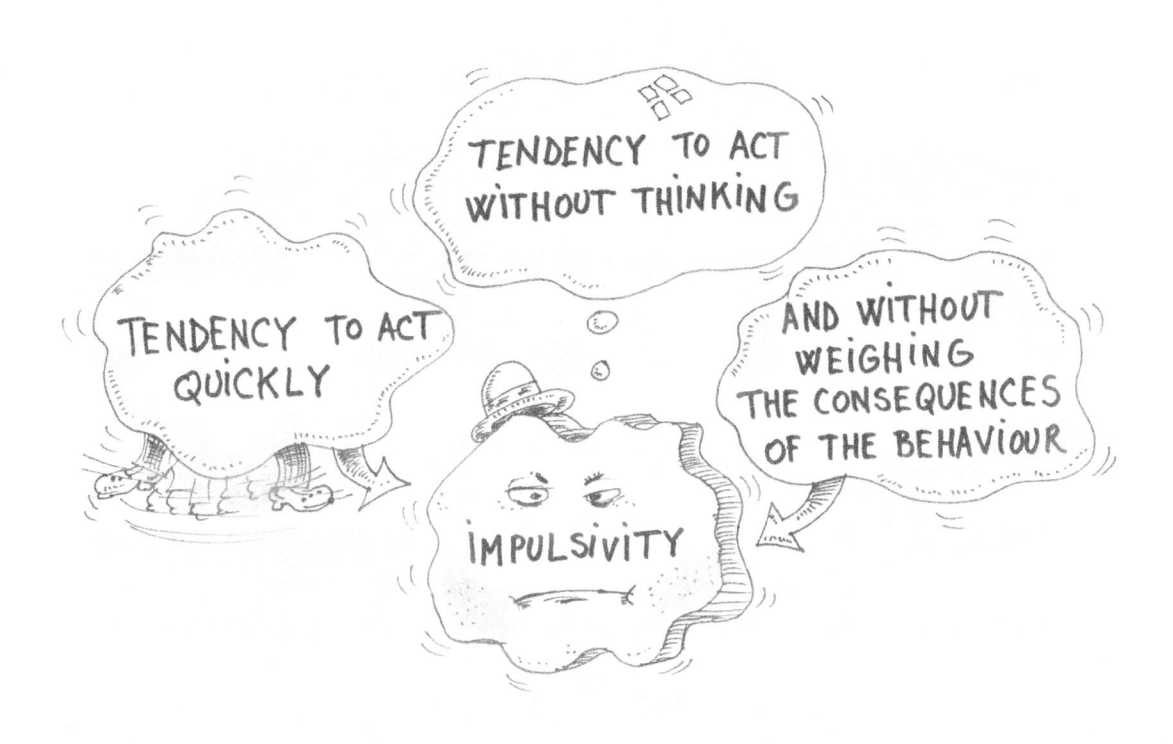

Impulsive behaviours or acts are considered to be ones that are not premeditated or considered in advance and over which the individual has little or no control. People who are unable to resist their urges and act on the spur of the moment usually feel very frustrated and disappointed with the consequences of their behaviour.

> *"Individuals with high levels of impulsivity experience difficulties, such as emotional instability and cognitive distractibility, engaging in behaviours that often result in undesirable outcomes"*
> -Gay, Schmidt, & Van der Linden, 2011

Take a moment to reflect on your behaviours and complete the "Am I impulsive" worksheet below to reflect your behaviours. The next worksheet, "Impulsivity tracker" can then be used to better understand your impulsive choices. After you have completed these worksheets use the "End of the Week Reflection" to deepen your understanding of situations where you are more likely to lose control. What are your regrets, and what are the consequences of your behaviour?

AM I IMPULSIVE?

There are 5 main components of Impulsivity:

- a tendency to make decisions to act too quickly
- a tendency to forgo planning and preparation
- a preference for small, immediate rewards
- a sense of not being in control of actions and choices
- feelings of guilt or regret about actions and choices afterwards.

Impulsivity can show up in many different areas of a person's life. It is possible to be impulsive in certain areas and not others, or it is possible to be impulsive or many or almost all areas of life. Use the worksheet below to explore areas of your life where impulsivity may show up:

How I spend money Example: buying things I can't afford/don't need	**How I interact with others** Examples: Interrupting Others, yelling when upset	**What I do for fun** Examples: watching pornography, canceling plans last-minute
How I make decisions at work Examples: responding too quickly, not asking for opinions of others	**How I take care of my body** Examples: overeating, staying up too late watching TV	**How I deal with stress** Examples: blaming others, drug or alcohol use

IMPULSIVITY TRACKER

For the next 7 days, make time at the end of your day to record any impulsive choices you regretted making that day, what factors lead up to making the choices, and what problems or consequences you experienced as a result. Use the example as a reference.

DATE/ TIME	IMPULSIVE CHOICE I REGRETTED LATER ON	WHAT LEAD UP TO MAKING THE CHOICE	WHAT PROBLMES OR CONSEQUENCES THE CHOICE CAUSED
2/21/19: after work	Drinking a 6 pack of beer	Stressful day at work, fight with wife	Fight with wife, guilt,

END OF WEEK REFLECTION

Look back at the impulsivity tracker for the past week, and use the prompts below to reflect on patterns you notice.

Looking back at your impulsive choices, what types of impulsive choices did you tend to make the most?

Were there certain times, situations, or circumstances where you were more likely to be impulsive?

What did you learn about yourself and your patterns that can help you be more successful in making different choices in these situations?

What types of problems or consequences did you experience, and what areas of your life were affected the most?

If you could travel back in time to right before you made some of these choices, what advice would you give yourself?

Impulses are just strong and often sudden urges to act. They can feel strong and urgent, but rarely represent actual emergencies. Just like the occasional emergency broadcasting tests on the television or radio, some may be incredibly loud and clear. Try to take impulses as a sign that your alert system is working well but remember that not all impulses are true emergencies that require us to take immediate action.

While our impulses can feel especially strong and urgent, learning to pause and think before acting on them is essential to helping our alert system function better. Each action and inaction helps to set the sensitivity of this alert system, almost like adjusting the settings. The more we do not react to "false alerts" or unhelpful impulses, the less we will experience these alerts, and the shorter and quieter they will become when they do arise.

Use our "False alarms" worksheet to understand and avoid reacting to your unhelpful urges.

FALSE ALARMS

False alarms are the unhelpful urges you get- the ones that lead to behaviours that cause problems for you and make you feel guilty later. Use the space provided to identify your false alarms and plan out how you will respond next time these happen. Remember that the less you act on the false alarm, the less it will go off, and the less loud it will be when it does.

False alarm urges me to: keep eating	**False alarm urges me to:**
It tries to trick me by: Mimicking hunger, pretending to be a need instead of a want	**It tries to trick me by:**
I can tell it's a false alarm because: It comes even after I've eaten a lot, and usually when I am stressed out or triggered	**I can tell it's a false alarm because:**
What I'll do next time it goes off: Remind myself I don't need to eat, stick to my scheduled meal plan	**What I'll do next time it goes off:**

False alarm urges me to:	**False alarm urges me to:**
It tries to trick me by:	**It tries to trick me by:**
I can tell it's a false alarm because:	**I can tell it's a false alarm because:**
What I'll do next time it goes off:	**What I'll do next time it goes off:**

The brain is constantly changing itself, forming new connections and pruning out the old ones in response to our behaviors. While acting on impulses strengthens the reward pathways in the brain and makes our impulses grow stronger, NOT acting on them weakens these same pathways and helps to form new, healthier pathways. Over time, these new pathways become more automatic, and we struggle with unhelpful impulses far less than we used to.

Use our "Rewiring the alarm system" worksheet:

REWIRING THE ALARM SYSTEM

When we respond to false alarms as if they are real, we are going to continue being disturbed by false alarms. The way to rewire your alarm system to be more accurate is to stop responding to false alarms as if they are real- or stop acting on urges as if they are "urgent". When you have an urge that feels urgent but you know is a "false alarm", you need to know what to NOT do, and what to do instead. Use the steps below to plan new responses to these false alarms.

	STOP DOING THIS		START DOING THIS INSTEAD
1	Being tricked by false alarms/non-urgent urges	1	Reminding yourself the urge is not urgent
2	Making decisions too quickly	2	Pausing before saying or doing anything
3	Thinking only about what would feel good right now	3	Considering how you will feel after the choice
4	Acting as if the only choice is to give in to the urge	4	Identifying alternative choices
5	Giving in and giving more power and control to the urge	5	Taking power and control back by making a different choice

Impulsive behaviour becomes an issue when:
- it can be an illegal act (e.g. stealing)
- it is costly, you often spend more than you can afford
- it is harmful either to oneself or others
- it damages your relationships with others
- it has negative consequences
- you feel guilty about what you have done and blame yourself for lack of ability to control your behaviour
- you are preoccupied with your desire to act impulsively and cannot resist your urges

Binge Eating Disorder or an Impulsive Binge Eating Problem?

In order to choose the right treatment for yourself, you need to know exactly what the problem is that you are dealing with. Is it an eating disorder or is it a poor relationship with food? Are you struggling with low self-esteem, poor emotional regulation, or are you confusing physical and emotional hunger? You will benefit from understanding exactly what you need to change, so that you can gain control over your impulsive overeating.

While most people overeat on occasion, when it becomes a pattern of behaviour that starts to cause serious consequences in a person's life, or to their physical or mental health, then they may be struggling with a serious condition called Binge Eating Disorder. In order for someone to be diagnosed with Binge Eating Disorder, the following criteria have to be met:

Criterion #1
The amount of food consumed within a defined period of time is more than most people would eat in the same time period. This occurs within a limited period of time, therefore, if an individual snacks or grazes all day long, then it would not be considered a binge eating episode. The amount of food involved would be considered excessive if it's more than a typical meal, and this is often associated with a lack of control, the inability to stop eating, or not being able to control the amount of food consumed. Some individuals may no longer try to control their eating habits and binge eating episodes might be planned.

Criterion #2
This criterion relates to the way in which food is eaten and the feelings that follow immediately afterwards. Binge eating is associated with at least three of the following:

- eating more rapidly than usual
- eating until uncomfortably full
- eating large amounts of food when not physically full

- eating alone because of being embarrassed about how much one is eating
- feeling disgusted with oneself, depressed, or very guilty afterwards

If three or more of these aspects are present, then criterion two is considered as being fulfilled. However, if only one or two aspects are present, then the criterion has not been fulfilled.

Criterion #3
This criterion relates specifically to the emotions that accompany episodes. Binge eating is characterized by marked distress. Individuals might feel depression, disgust, shame, guilt, or any similar negative emotions.

Criterion #4
This criterion relates to the frequency of episodes. Binge eating is considered to be taking place if it happens at least once a week for at least three months. The mild range involves 1–3 episodes per week, the moderate range involves 4–7 episodes per week, and the severe range involves 8–13 episodes. If there are 14 or more episodes in a week, then the case is considered extreme.

Criterion #5
This criterion relates to behaviour that is not considered part of Binge Eating Disorder. It's not associated with the recurrent use of inappropriate compensatory behaviour to make up for or reverse the effects of the episode (unlike bulimia, where binging is followed by purging or the use of laxatives).

A 2007 study of Americans found that Binge Eating Disorder is approximately 3 times more prevalent than Anorexia and Bulimia, and that 3.5% of women and 2% of men reported having a Binge Eating Disorder at some point in their lives (Biological Psychiatry, accessed on nationaleatingdisorders.org).

If you suspect that you might be suffering from an eating disorder like Binge Eating Disorder, it is strongly recommended that you seek help from a licensed health or mental health professional. Eating disorders are serious conditions that can have severe impacts on your health. People who suffer from one eating disorder are more likely to suffer from another eating disorder at some point later in their lives.

This book is in no way a substitute for professional treatment but can be a helpful tool for those who are in treatment, so that they can continue their progress outside of sessions. It is also helpful for those who do not have an eating disorder but feel that their overeating has become problematic for them in some way.

Part 2 - WHY Binge Eating Occurs & What Causes It

> *"Do not let circumstances control you. You change your circumstances."*
> *~ Jackie Chan ~*

5 Predispositions of Impulsivity

Let's take a closer look at the five main predispositions of impulsivity. You can use the knowledge of them to create a better plan to manage your impulsive behaviours.

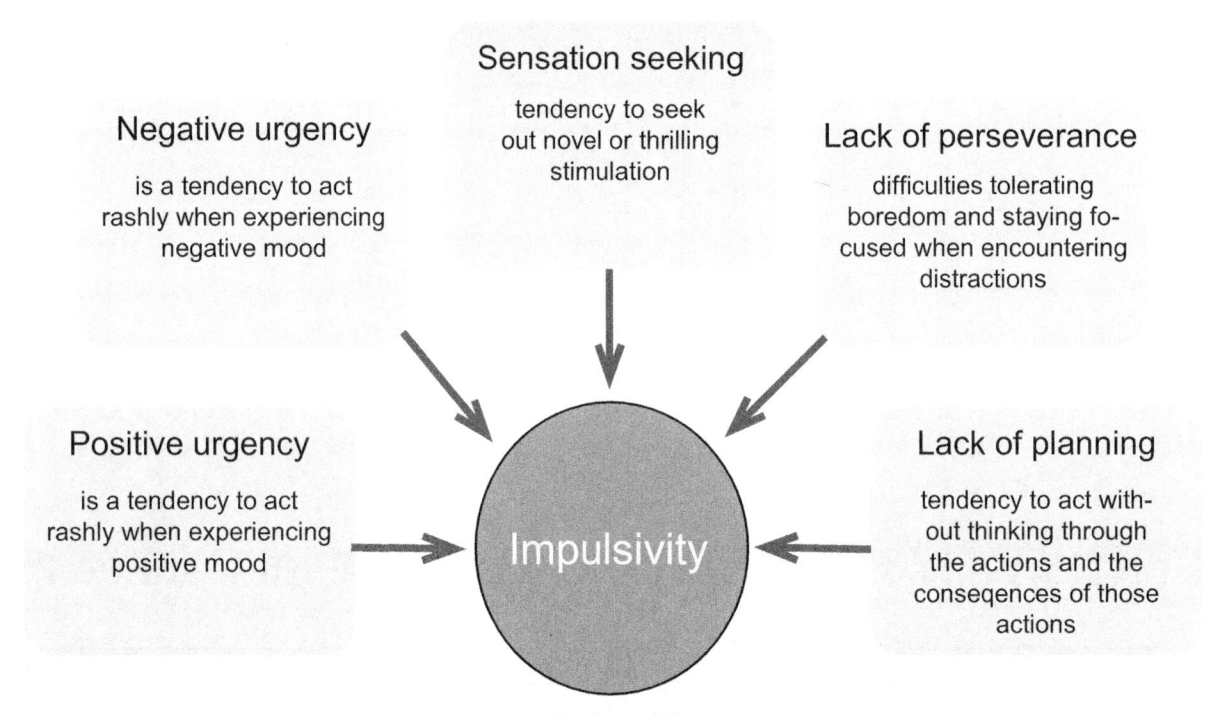

Sensation seeking
tendency to seek out novel or thrilling stimulation

Negative urgency
is a tendency to act rashly when experiencing negative mood

Lack of perseverance
difficulties tolerating boredom and staying focused when encountering distractions

Positive urgency
is a tendency to act rashly when experiencing positive mood

Impulsivity

Lack of planning
tendency to act without thinking through the actions and the conseqences of those actions

It has been suggested that there is no single personality trait that underlies the disposition for impulsive actions (Dick et al., 2010). It has been proposed that five dispositions underlie this trait. These are positive urgency, negative urgency, sensation seeking, lack of planning, and lack of perseverance. (Whiteside & Lynam, 2001).

Are you more likely to impulsively overeat when you experience positive or negative emotions?

Positive urgency and negative urgency as experienced by individuals are based on emotions (Dick et al., 2010). Positive urgency is a tendency to act rashly when experiencing positive mood and negative urgency is the tendency to act rashly when experiencing negative mood (Dick et al., 2010). Individuals high in urgency might have trouble resisting temptations and cravings (Johnson & Kim, 2011).

In a 2012 study (2), negative urgency was significantly associated with two measures of dysregulated eating (binge eating and emotional eating). The findings from this study suggest that negative urgency likely increases the risk of developing binge eating and emotional eating.

It is likely that interactions between the risk factors are relevant to the development of dysregulated eating and may explain a larger percentage of variance than main effects alone. In another study, anger, as compared to other negative emotions, is shown to play a major role in emotionally elicited binge eating. Binge eaters described anger or frustration prior to a binge 42% of the time but sadness or depression only 16% of the time (Arnow et al., 1992).

Take a moment and reflect on your impulsive overeating:

How do you feel just before you reach out for your temptations?

Do you experience positive or negative emotions?

Are you stressed?

Did you have an argument with someone? Write down the recent incident.

Were there times in the past when you experienced these emotions but didn't binge?

It may be that individuals high on negative urgency are more likely to develop binge eating versus another kind of impulsive behaviour. For example, those who are diagnosed with kleptomania – an impulse control disorder – often do it because of the thrill of it or pleasure associated with it, rather than because they need items and cannot afford them.

What is sensation seeking?

When we say sensation seeking, we refer to the tendency to seek out novel or thrilling stimulation. Often, such stimulating activities might include fast driving or engaging in fights, activities that put the individuals involved and people close to them at risk. Sensation seeking, however, might provide a barrier against high levels of anxiety and dysfunctional avoidance (such as thought suppression) (Gay et al., 2011).

Think about yourself; are you looking for new and exciting activities in your life? If so, do you engage in safe and exciting activities or are you more likely to do something reckless that might be potentially dangerous?

Lack of planning

Lack of planning (or lack of premeditation) is considered to be the tendency to act without thinking through the consequences of these actions (Johnson & Kim, 2011). Individuals experiencing deficits in the area of planning often act without thinking about the effects of their behaviour on themselves and others (Johnson & Kim, 2011). It is considered that psychological factors associated with heightened impulsivity are a decreased level of control and a lesser degree of planning in impulsive acts (Parry & Lindsay, 2003).

Think about your attempts to diet and to manage your weight; what were your stumbling blocks?

Were there times when you didn't shop well (forgot to buy greens and ended up with cookies and chips)?

When you don't take your lunch with you to work, what choices to you make to eat out?

Do you plan what to eat when you go to a birthday party? Or do you plan to have something small and healthy to eat beforehand so you are not starving?

> **What is on your shopping list?**
>
>

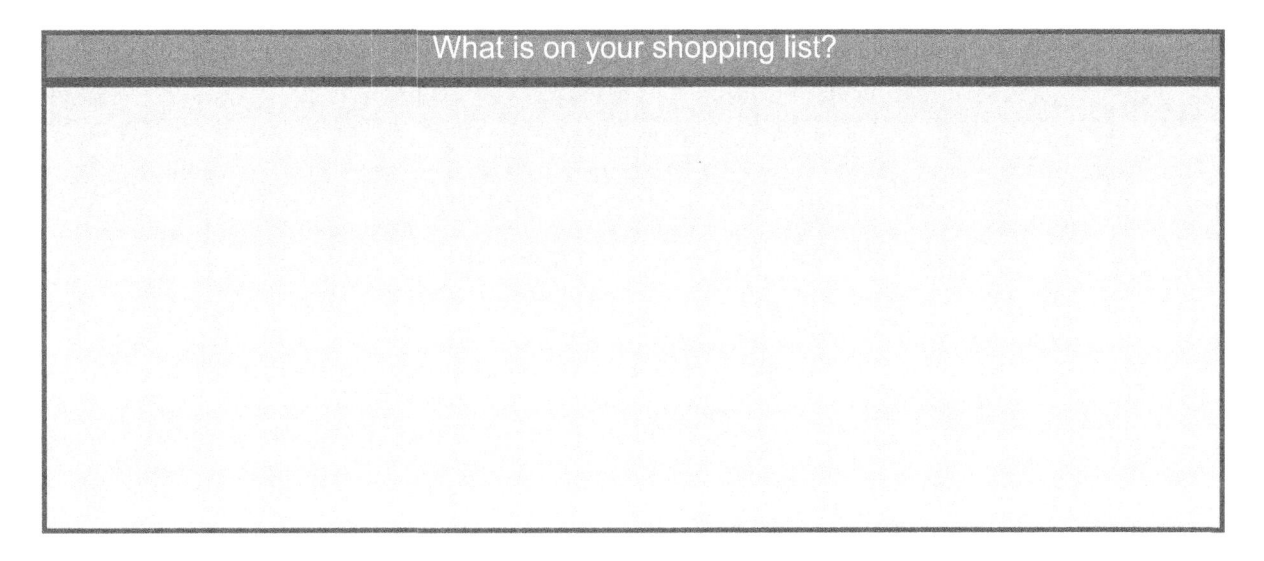

Lack of perseverance

People who have difficulty tolerating boredom and staying focused when encountering distractions appear to experience lack of perseverance. This suggests that lack of perseverance might be related to 'resistance to proactive interference' (Dick et al., 2010). In other words, individuals who experience difficulties in this domain might not be able to attend to tasks that are perceived as boring or difficult (Johnson & Kim, 2011). But we can't talk about perseverance without discussing dopamine...

What is Dopamine

Dopamine is a neurotransmitter that helps control the brain's reward and pleasure centres. It is also responsible for regulative movement and emotional response.

Dopamine enables you not only to identify a reward but to take steps towards it. For example, you are not just identifying and registering your favourite food, let's say a muffin, but you take the steps to get up and move to the kitchen, then you pick the muffin up and eat it (Arnow et al., 1992).

Jean Wiecha and her colleagues have emphasised that we need to shift our focus from obesity to empowering children to want healthy food and to learn to love the feeling and consequences of being active and fit and eating well (Wiecha et al., 2012).

Ask yourself:

Do I persevere despite difficulties and setbacks, or do I tend to throw in the towel and call it quits when faced with a challenge or adversity?

Do you procrastinate? If so, why?

What do you do to motivate yourself?

> **What makes some people able to keep pushing and complete a task while others habitually don't follow through?**

> **Does this mean that dopamine helps me to stay motivated and achieve my goals? How can I turn it on?**

Researchers believe that you can increase your production of dopamine by changing your attitude and behaviour. They refer to it as the 'reward molecule' – higher levels of dopamine have been linked to forming lifelong habits, such as perseverance.

> *"Goals allow you to control the direction of change in your favour".*
> *~ Brian Tracy ~*

Dr. Joe Tsiend said that this discovery helps us to speed up the process of forming good habits and possibly removing the bad ones.

MY MOTIVATION TO CHANGE

Write down your three main reasons to change your eating habits.

Step 1: I binge eat because... (e.g. It makes me feel better, helps to deal with boredom)	Step 2: Bad things happen as a result of my binge, such as... (e.g. I feel disgusted afterwards)

Step 1: I think quitting binge eating would be hard because... (e.g. I find it hard to control myself)	Step 1: My life will be better in many ways if I stop binging because... (e.g. I will feel better about myself, maintain my weight)

My main reasons to change my binge eating:

1. _____

2. _____

3. _____

CHANGE BELIEFS

While it is normal to have some doubts and conflicting thoughts about change, we need to work on strengthening these 3 beliefs, as they are what will keep us motivated to continue working towards a healthier lifestyle. Use the space below to reflect on these 3 beliefs, and to identify "reminders" you need when you begin to doubt these beliefs:

Change is NECESSARY: the belief that we need to change because of the consequences associated with not changing.

Change is POSSIBLE: the belief that we are capable of changing, either because we have the skills/abilities or a strong belief that we can develop them.

Change will be WORTH IT: the belief that making this change will result in some meaningful long-term reward or benefit to ourselves, our lives, or our futures.

1. Why is it necessary for you to make changes to your eating habits? What is the cost of not changing?

When you start to feel less confident that change is necessary, what do you need to remind yourself of?

2. What skills and abilities have helped you make positive changes to your eating habits?

3. What will the long-term rewards or benefits of changing your eating habits be? If you are successful, what will it mean for you, your life, and your future?

When you start to doubt whether changing your eating habits will be "worth it", what do you need to remind yourself of?

Ask yourself:

How should I change my attitude?

How can I learn to persevere despite feeling bored or frustrated?

What new habits do I need to form to help me feel better?

FINDING YOUR PATTERNS

Be curious about your eating habits. Complete "Finding your Patterns" to understand your eating patterns.

Planned Food		Food Consumed		Daily Evaluation/ Notes
Date:				
Breakfast:	1 pack instant oatmeal and banana	Breakfast:	1 pack instant oatmeal and banana	Overall evaluation of eating today: ☐ Poor ☐ Fair ☐ Good ☐ Excellent
Lunch:	Chicken wrap and side salad	Lunch:	Chicken wrap and side salad	
Snack/s:	Almond snack pack	Snack/s:	Almond snack pack	Reason: Had one extra snack but also went on additional 30 minute walk.
Dinner:	1/2 c pasta with marinara and 2 sausages	Dinner:	1/2 c pasta with marinara and 2 sausages	
Dessert:	1/2 c raspberry sorbet	Dessert:	1/2 c raspberry sorbet	
Date:				
Breakfast:		Breakfast:		Overall evaluation of eating today: ☐ Poor ☐ Fair ☐ Good ☐ Excellent
Lunch:		Lunch:		
Snack/s:		Snack/s:		Reason:
Dinner:		Dinner:		
Dessert:		Dessert:		

FINDING YOUR PATTERNS CONTINUED

Be curious about your eating habits. Complete "Finding your Patterns" to understand your eating patterns.

Planned Food		Food Consumed		Daily Evaluation/ Notes
Date:				
Breakfast:		Breakfast:		Overall evaluation of eating today: ☐ Poor ☐ Fair ☐ Good ☐ Excellent
Lunch:		Lunch:		
Snack/s:		Snack/s:		Reason:
Dinner:		Dinner:		
Dessert:		Dessert:		
Date:				
Breakfast:		Breakfast:		Overall evaluation of eating today: ☐ Poor ☐ Fair ☐ Good ☐ Excellent
Lunch:		Lunch:		
Snack/s:		Snack/s:		Reason:
Dinner:		Dinner:		
Dessert:		Dessert:		

FINDING YOUR PATTERNS CONTINUED

Be curious about your eating habits. Complete "Finding your Patterns" to understand your eating patterns.

Planned Food	Food Consumed	Daily Evaluation/ Notes
Date:		
Breakfast:	Breakfast:	Overall evaluation of eating today: ☐ Poor ☐ Fair ☐ Good ☐ Excellent
Lunch:	Lunch:	
Snack/s:	Snack/s:	Reason:
Dinner:	Dinner:	
Dessert:	Dessert:	
Date:		
Breakfast:	Breakfast:	Overall evaluation of eating today: ☐ Poor ☐ Fair ☐ Good ☐ Excellent
Lunch:	Lunch:	
Snack/s:	Snack/s:	Reason:
Dinner:	Dinner:	
Dessert:	Dessert:	

FINDING YOUR PATTERNS CONTINUED

Next, review your food diary and answer the questions below to work on identifying some of your patterns:

How much and how often are you eating?

Who are you usually eating with during the times when you overeat?

What types of food are you eating too much of and which type of foods are you not eating enough of?

When are you most likely to overeat?

What other patterns do you notice during times when you overeat?

Great job! Knowing your patterns of overeating will help you pay closer attention and plan more for times and situations when you are most likely to overeat.

RETHINKING NEGATIVE IMPACTS

Use the left-hand column to make a list of all of the negative ways that overeating has impacted you, then list the "ripple effects" of these impacts. In the right-hand column, re-think these impacts as potential positive impacts of eating healthier. See example for reference.

	OVEREATING — Negative Impacts and Ripples		HEALTHY EATING + Positive Impacts and Ripples
Impact:	Lowered self-esteem due to weight gain	Impact:	Weight loss and higher self-esteem
Ripples:	Avoid dating Self-concious in public Wear clothes I don't like More quiet in groups	Ripples:	More likely to date More social and active More pride in appearance Less afraid to speak up
Impact:		Impact:	
Ripples:		Ripples:	
Impact:		Impact:	
Ripples:		Ripples:	
Impact:		Impact:	
Ripples:		Ripples:	
Impact:		Impact:	
Ripples:		Ripples:	

Pain & Pleasure Principle

Many of our impulses are based on the pain/pleasure principle. This principle refers to a set of evolutionary impulses that all humans have, causing us to seek pleasure and avoid pain. Intended to help our species survive, these impulses can be intense and difficult not to act on.

Our impulses to pull our hands away from a hot surface, or to run away from danger are examples of the pain principle in action. Our sexual drive is an example of the pleasure principle in action. Other more modern pleasures like pornography, processed foods, drugs, alcohol, shopping, or gambling, also illustrate this principle. But we can argue that these types of pleasures have less of an evolutionary function and are also more likely to result in long-term pain.

This paradox illustrates the way that our pain/pleasure principle hasn't evolved to mirror modern reality. In many instances, things that bring immediate pleasure (like unhealthy foods, drugs, or alcohol), often bring more pain and suffering in the long term.

The pleasures derived from overeating are short-term - we overeat and then are hungry again within hours, but the long-term consequences to our health can be deadly. This is why, in order to overcome our problem with overeating and make a lasting change, we need to learn ways to recognise and manage our food impulses.

Each time you crave unhealthy food or have an urge to keep eating when you are not really hungry or know you've had enough, you have a choice to either feed the impulse or starve it. The more you feed it, the bigger and stronger it will grow.
But the less you feed it, the weaker and smaller it will become.

Emotional Vs Physical Hunger

You might wonder where emotional hunger comes from… The source can be many different places, but usually represents some area of our self or our life where we feel unfulfilled, unhappy, or empty.

While physical hunger comes from an empty stomach, emotional hunger can come from an empty relationship, a dissatisfying job, or unhappiness with some aspect of ourselves or our lives. Take a moment to ask yourself where your emotional hunger might be coming from.

What area of your life feels unfulfilled?

What kinds of emotions and problems cause you to turn to food?

Just like swallowing a pill or some water wouldn't satiate our physical hunger, food will not satiate our emotional hunger… it is not the sustenance that this hunger needs to be healthy, nourished, and strong.

What kind of sustenance does your emotional hunger need?

I'M NOT HUNGRY, I'M...

Use the space below to describe times when you eat for reasons other than being physically hungry. Then, use the spaces below to write ideas about other things you can do instead of eat during these times.

I'm not hungry, I'm…	I'm not hungry, I'm…
Other ways I can cope or respond to this:	Other ways I can cope or respond to this:

I'm not hungry, I'm…	I'm not hungry, I'm…
Other ways I can cope or respond to this:	Other ways I can cope or respond to this:

I'm not hungry, I'm…	I'm not hungry, I'm…
Other ways I can cope or respond to this:	Other ways I can cope or respond to this:

DAILY PROGRESS CHECKLIST

Today I...	Check	Comment

I have noticed that I am better at _____

_____

I am still working on _____

Tomorrow I will try _____

When we think about our life satisfaction, we can identify that there are several different areas of life to consider. Psychologists often refer to these different areas as 'life domains'. Examples of life domains include:

Physical health: our general health including our health conditions, sleep, nutritional habits, and generally how our body feels and functions.

Mental health: Mental health includes how happy or unhappy we are, and how in control of ourselves, our thoughts and behaviours we feel. It also includes how we feel about ourselves - our self-concept, self-esteem, and self-image.

Social relationships: Our friends, family, and people we interact with all comprise our social sector. How deeply we feel connected to these people, how often we see them, and how well we communicate with them all plays into our social life domain.

Occupational: this includes work, but also educational settings or volunteer settings and more importantly how effective we feel in these occupational roles, how in sync we feel these roles are with our interests and abilities, and generally how satisfied we are in these roles.

Recreational: This domain refers to all leisure activities outside of our occupational roles and can include hobbies, activities, and things we enjoy doing alone or with others. Having meaningful recreational activities that we enjoy is an important part of balancing our lives.

Belief system: This domain includes all of our larger beliefs about ourselves, our purpose, and our futures. It can include religious or spiritual beliefs for some but does not necessarily have to be spiritual or religious in nature. It also reflects our values or guiding principles about what is most important to us.

Thinking about each of these domains can sometimes provide clarity to people who wonder where their emotional hunger might be coming from.

EXPECTATION VS. REALITY

Use this worksheet to write down some of the unhelpful expectations you have about food before overeating, and then to compare these to your actual experience during times when you have overeaten.

Before I start eating, I expect… that I will be able to stop after one serving.	**Before I start eating, I expect…**
But in reality: I usually end up eating the whole box.	**But in reality:**

Before I start eating, I expect…	**Before I start eating, I expect…**
But in reality:	**But in reality:**

Before I start eating, I expect…	**Before I start eating, I expect…**
But in reality:	**But in reality:**

> Which of these life domains do you feel least satisfied in? During times when there were stressful events happening in these areas of your life, did you notice that your overeating was worse?

Consider making a list of activities and actions you could take in each of these life areas to improve your satisfaction in this area or to reduce stress in this area.

Stress

Stress can be present in any area of our life and can have an impact on how we feel, how we think, and how we behave. Stress creates changes in our brains and our nervous system. Cortisol and adrenaline are released in the brain, which over time, can cause a multitude of health and mental health issues to develop or worsen. Stress also changes the way our mind (the thinking part of our brain) works, and we become much more likely to struggle with strong impulses when under stress. This is because stress impacts the frontal lobes of the brain, which are responsible for helping us make decisions and think things all the way through.

In certain situations, stress can be motivating - we may put in extra work in order to meet an upcoming deadline or we may be motivated by stress to make big changes (like deciding to pick up this book to work on overeating). This is a perfect example of the pain principle in action - stress is a type of psychological pain that we try to take actions to avoid or guard against.

Some of these actions are beneficial, but others are harmful and create more stress in the long-term. Any type of addictive behaviour may reduce immediate stress but cause more stress in the long run. Overeating can be a way that people cope with and relieve stress but the physical and mental health effects that come from it cause more suffering.

Stress isn't always motivating. There are times when high levels of stress exceed our ability to cope and these are times when we are more likely to turn to behaviours that have a high dopamine reward, like overeating or using drugs or alcohol.

Taking steps to reduce stress means using a two-fold approach:

#1 - The first part is to take actions to change or eliminate the source of stress (which is also called a stressor). Examples of this could be to set better boundaries with co-workers to reduce work stress, sleeping more to reduce health stress, or making a budget to reduce financial stress.

#2 - The second part of stress-management is to learn more effective ways to cope with and reduce stress. Activities like attending counselling, journaling, exercising, and meditation are examples of coping skills that are helpful to many people in reducing stress levels.

Prioritising these types of activities is essential to overcoming overeating, especially since many people describe overeating as a way to deal with stress. Stress is also important in maintaining healthy lifestyle choices, as research has shown that stress is one of the biggest contributors to relapse in people recovering from addiction.

Ask yourself...

What actions can you take to address and resolve the sources of your stress? What healthy activities help alleviate and reduce your stress levels, and how can you make time for these in the coming weeks?

What healthy activities help alleviate and reduce your stress levels, and how can you make time for these in the coming weeks?

Emotions

Besides stress, another common component of overeating is our emotions.

Anger, as compared to other negative emotions, possibly plays a major role in emotional binge eating. In one study, binge eaters described anger or frustration prior to a binge 42% of the time but sadness or depression only 16% of the time. Because food is central to culture, it is important to note that there can be differences across cultures about people's eating habits, as well as emotional triggers for eating. For instance, one study of eight European nations found that the experiences of anger and joy were more prevalent than fear and sadness, and that these emotions more commonly preceded instances of overeating in these nations.

For some, overeating happens when they experience joy - think celebrations, parties, and special occasions. For others, difficult emotions like fear or sadness may lead to overeating - think about the cliché image of a woman eating an entire gallon of ice-cream to mend a broken heart. For others still, a variety of emotions may lead to overeating.

Ask yourself…

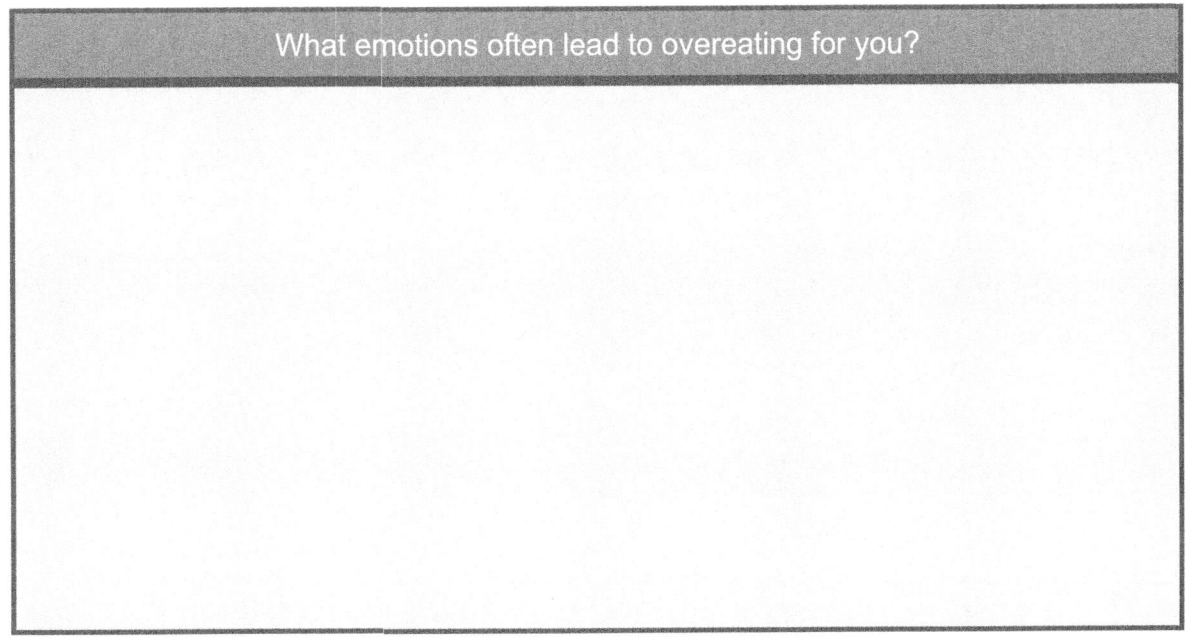

What emotions often lead to overeating for you?

A recent study found that emotions play a far more important role in influencing your eating habits than gender difference, self-restraint, or weight status. Another important aspect of recovery is to learn new strategies of responding to and coping with your emotions.

> "You cannot control what happens to you, but you can control your attitude toward what happens to you, and in that, you will be mastering change rather than allowing it to master you."
> ~ Brian Tracy ~

For those who eat when they are happy, what are other healthier ways that you can celebrate or reward yourself?

If you tend to overeat when at social events, what are some other social settings or activities that do not revolve around food?

What about you? What strategy would you choose?

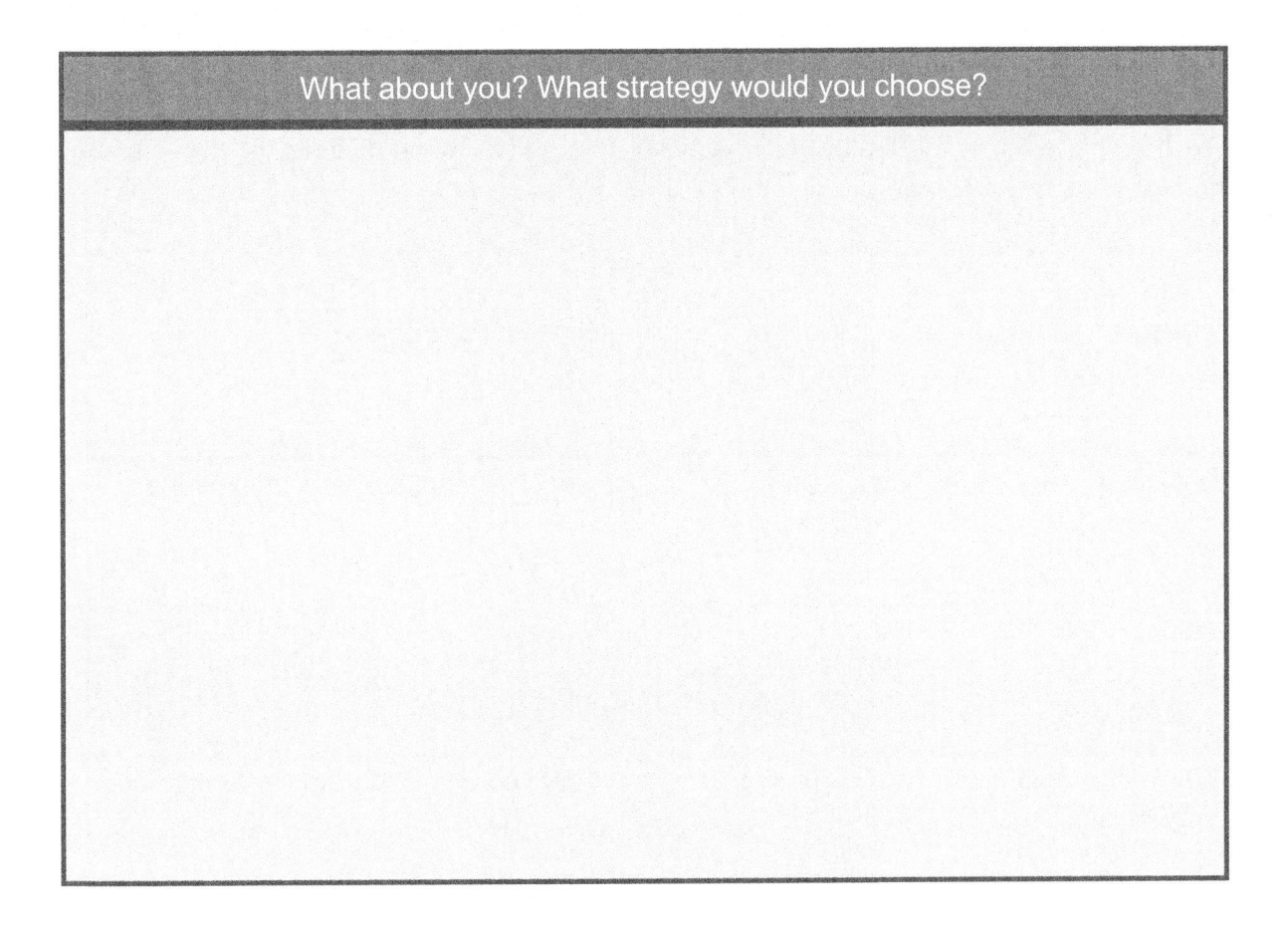

For those who eat when they are afraid, finding ways to manage your anxiety may be an important part of recovery for you. Some strategies for managing anxiety include physical activity, switching your attention away from anxious thoughts to whatever you are doing in the moment, using breathing and relaxation exercises, or guided meditations.

For those who eat when sad, finding other activities that help to lift your mood may be important. Some examples are spending time with friends, listening to a favourite album, getting outdoors, or going out to do something you love.

EMOTIONAL RESPONSES

Use the space below to identify skilful ways to respond to these difficult emotions, using the example as a reference.

Emotion I struggle with: Anger
How I have responded in the past: Ruminated, blamed others, lashed out
What I can focus on instead: How to prevent this from reoccurring
What I can do differently in response: Communicating my concerns and needs

Emotion I struggle with:
How I have responded in the past:
What I can focus on instead:
What I can do differently in response:

Emotion I struggle with:
How I have responded in the past:
What I can focus on instead:
What I can do differently in response:

Emotion I struggle with:
How I have responded in the past:
What I can focus on instead:
What I can do differently in response:

EMOTIONAL CARE-GIVING

Part of learning to control our impulses means we need to get better at dealing with difficult emotions that we have used food to cope with. Use the worksheet below to identify emotional needs and more effective ways to respond to these needs.

EMOTION What am I feeling?	EMOTIONAL NEEDS What does this emotion need?	EFFECTIVE RESPONSES What should I do?
SADNESS	I.e.: comfort, support	I.e.: call a friend, journal
BOREDOM	I.e.: entertainment, activity	I.e.: go for a walk, make plans
ANGER	I.e.: a break, time to think	I.e.: take a break, think it through
FEAR	I.e.: comfort, courage	I.e.: face my fear
JOY	I.e.: celebration, reward	I.e.: share good news with a friend
LONELINESS	I.e.: support, connection	I.e.: make plans with friends

When we choose an alternative action in response to these emotions, we begin to break down the association we have developed between emotions and food. This is essential for most people working to develop healthier eating habits.

There are five stages of dealing with feelings that you may be familiar with…

1. Recognition:
If you feel restless, you can recognise this feeling by saying:
"I know that there is a restlessness in me."
You can also recognise bodily sensations:
"I am feeling fidgety, bored, and frustrated."

2. Acceptance:
If you feel restless, do not deny it.
You can accept what is present here, "I accept that I feel restless right now."

3. Embracing:
Holding a difficult emotion with empathy is much more effective than punishing or criticising yourself for having the feeling.

4. Looking deeply:
When you feel calm again you can look at this restlessness to see what really caused it.
What are the beliefs and assumptions that underly this restlessness?
Maybe one of the unhelpful thinking patterns is causing this feeling?

5. Insight:
Understanding the many causes of restlessness is where insight comes from.
This may be experienced as a feeling:
"No wonder I feel this way now, because of this circumstance and the way I interpret it I feel this way."
"I know what to do and I know if I engage in the unhelpful behaviour it will lead to bad consequences."
"It is a feeling and it is going to pass. It cannot hurt me."

Notice the difference between accepting the thoughts and trying to suppress them.

You can allow the thoughts to be present and not do anything about them. You can just wait for them to pass instead of trying to get rid of them.

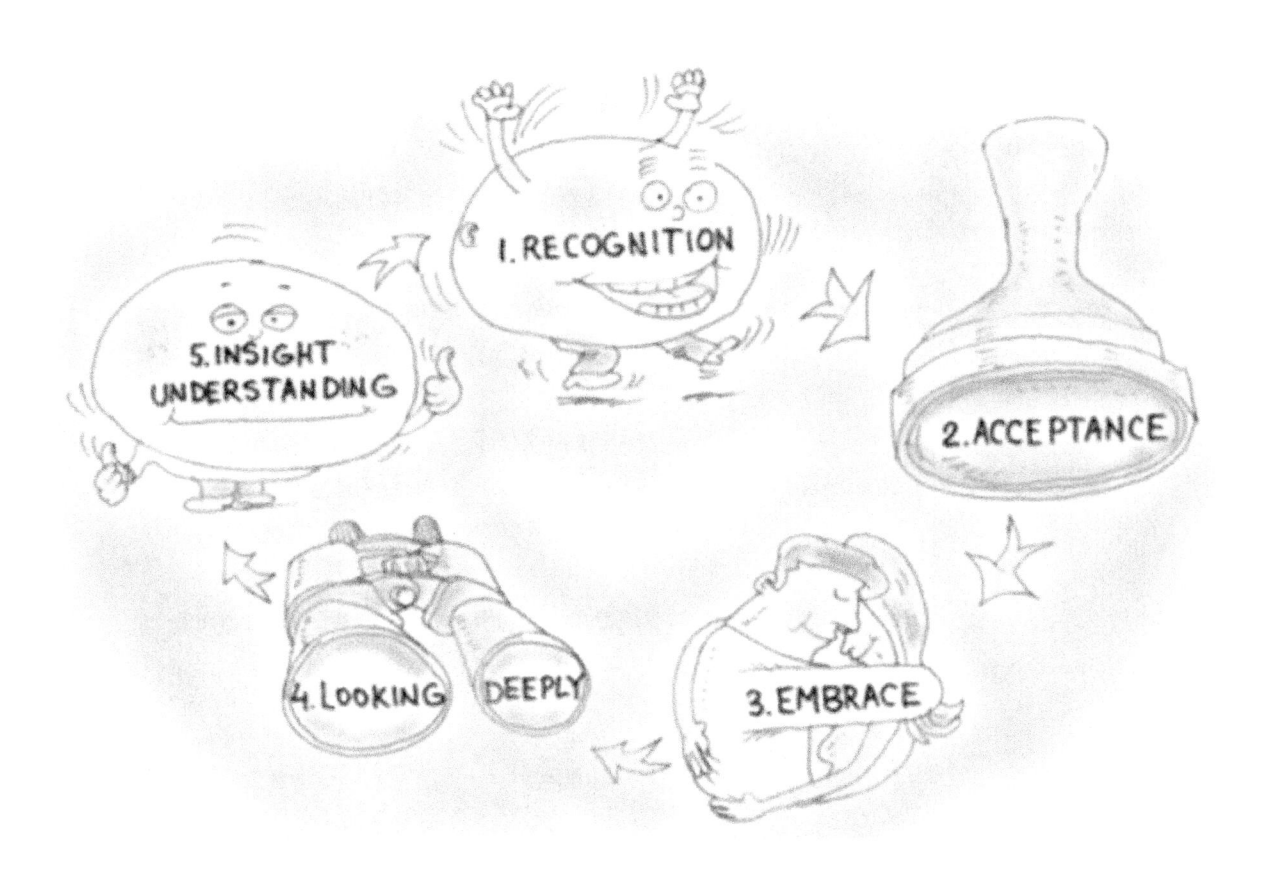

TO DO OR NOT TO DO...

Use the space below to identify what thought, feeling, or impulse you will work on responding mindfully to and to track your use of mindfulness when this comes up. After you have had at least 3 successes in using the skill and not acting on the urge, complete the Reflection portion below.

Instead of doing something or making choices when an impulse, thought or feeling comes up practice mindfulness by following these 5 steps.

1. **Recognise** it is there and give it a name
2. **Accept** it is there for now
3. **Embrace** it by inviting it in instead of trying to make it leave
4. **Look deeply** at it to better understand it and where it comes from
5. **Find the lesson** it has for you and use it to move forward

THOUGHT, FEELING, OR URGE	PRACTICE #1 Date/Situation/Success	PRACTICE #2 Date/Situation Success	PRACTICE #3 Date/Situation Success
I.e.: Urge to overeat	**Date:** 2/21/19 **Situation:** catered lunch at work **Successful in not acting on the urge?** Yes No	**Date:** 2/21/19 **Situation:** dinner at mother's house **Successful in not acting on the urge?** Yes No	**Date:** 2/21/19 **Situation:** offered fast food by friend **Successful in not acting on the urge?** Yes No
	Date: **Situation:** **Successful in not acting on the urge?** Yes No	**Date:** **Situation:** **Successful in not acting on the urge?** Yes No	**Date:** **Situation:** **Successful in not acting on the urge?** Yes No
	Date: **Situation:** **Successful in not acting on the urge?** Yes No	**Date:** **Situation:** **Successful in not acting on the urge?** Yes No	**Date:** **Situation:** **Successful in not acting on the urge?** Yes No

TO DO OR NOT TO DO... CONTINUED

Reflection: Answer the questions below about your experience using mindfulness in response to the urge, thought, or feeling that you identified. Use the examples provided as a reference.

What changes in your body or mind helped you recognize this thought/feeling/urge when it came up? (I.e.: empty feeling in stomach, thoughts of food, desire to get up for more)

What did you notice was different when you were "accepting" the urge/feeling/thought instead of trying to control it? (I.e.: it felt strange and different, but freed up a lot of energy

Is there a new way of thinking about this urge/feeling/thought that makes it easier to embrace it? (I.e.: thinking that each time I experience it, I am getting stronger)

Was there anything new that you were able to understand about this urge/feeling/thought or where it comes from? (I.e.: It just sort of goes away on it's own, even if I do nothing)

What "lesson" did you learn from this experience and how can you use this in the future? (I.e.: there is a social aspect of this behaviour- I am more likely to have strong urges to overeat when I am with people I am most comfortable with)

What is another urge/thought/feeling that you want to practice using these steps on? (I.e.: I want to start practicing using these steps when I feel overwhelmed, since this is another internal trigger for me)

MODERATE EATING

When we are working towards making healthier eating decisions, moderation is a keyword that we need to keep in mind. Foods we commonly overeat (usually unhealthy foods high in calories and low in nutrients) are usually foods we need to think carefully about moderating.

Foods to Moderate (Unhealthy foods)

TRIGGER FOOD	PORTION/AMOUNT	HOW OFTEN
Example: potato chips	1 small bag	2x / week or less

Replacement Foods (Healthy alternatives)

TRIGGER FOOD	REPLACEMENT FOOD	PORTION / FREQUENCY
Example: potato chips	Veggie Chips	1 serving per day

Example of daily meal plan

BREAKFAST	LUNCH	DINNER	SNACKS
Example: instant oatmeal, banana, coffee	Turkey wrap, apple, 24 oz water	6 oz grilled chicken, 1/2 c rice, 1 c broccoli	Veggie chips, Peanut butter crackers

IDENTIFYING AND DEALING WITH TRIGGERS

We need to pay attention to our triggers: external (such as smell) and internal (such as memory). It has been suggested that when your journey to success begins it might be better for you to avoid triggers. For example, if this is your first week of trying to manage your binge eating, it might be better to cancel that open-buffet dinner with your relatives.

PHASE I

Potential trigger	What to do
Jane's birthday on Wednesday	I will plan a meeting offsite

However, when you feel a bit stronger and have practised resisting your urges and temptations, prepare for being exposed to those triggers but without reacting or having to binge straight away.

PHASE II

Trigger	Plan of attack
Jane's birthday on Wednesday	I will have breakfast, eat healthy snacks, do my visualisations exercise, remember to stay relaxed and remind myself that I want to be fit more than I want a slice of cake.

IDENTIFYING YOUR TRIGGERS FOR UNHELPFUL IMPULSE BEHAVIOUR

We need to know what happens when we are more likely to do something impulsive.
You can learn to identify when you are more likely to engage in your impulsive behaviour.
Often you will find that it happens automatically.
Look at the picture below and try to answer these questions the best that you can:

Imagine yourself in an irresistible situation

Fill out all the boxes on this page that apply to your experience of irresistible situations.

Scenario #1

I am likely to	drink beer
When I/then I do	think about upcoming exams, then I usually feel stressed
or I hear	
or I smell	
or I see	and when I see my friends going to a pub
Afterwards, I feel	horrible, I don't have enough time to study, and I have a splitting headache

Scenario #2

I am likely to	
When I/then I do	
or I hear	
or I smell	
or I see	
Afterwards, I feel	

Scenario #3

I am likely to	
When I/then I do	
or I hear	
or I smell	
or I see	
Afterwards, I feel	

Scenario #4

I am likely to	
When I/then I do	
or I hear	
or I smell	
or I see	
Afterwards, I feel	

Triggers

Food triggers refer to feelings, people, places, things, and situations we have come to associate with food. We all have food associations, like connecting ice-cream with hot days, popcorn with movies, or cake with birthdays. For people who struggle with over-eating, these food triggers can be especially powerful, leading to strong urges to over-eat.

For this reason, it is important to think more about what your food triggers are.

Food triggers can be internal - related to your thoughts or emotions. They can also be external, related to people, places, things, and situations in our environment.

External triggers include things, people, places, and situations in our environment that we have built food associations around. These can include specific types of events (like parties) or places (like restaurants or bars), specific people (who we tend to overeat with) or situations (like sunny days, baseball games, catered work meetings, and so on).

You have already learned and thought about some of your internal triggers, but what are your external triggers?

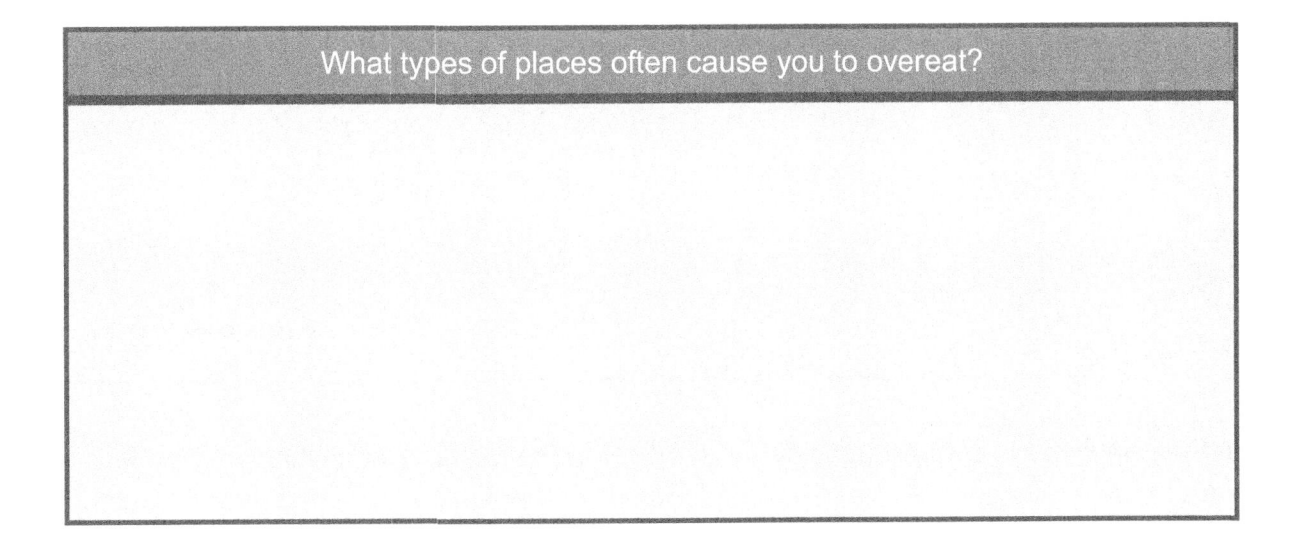

What types of places often cause you to overeat?

Who do you tend to overeat with?

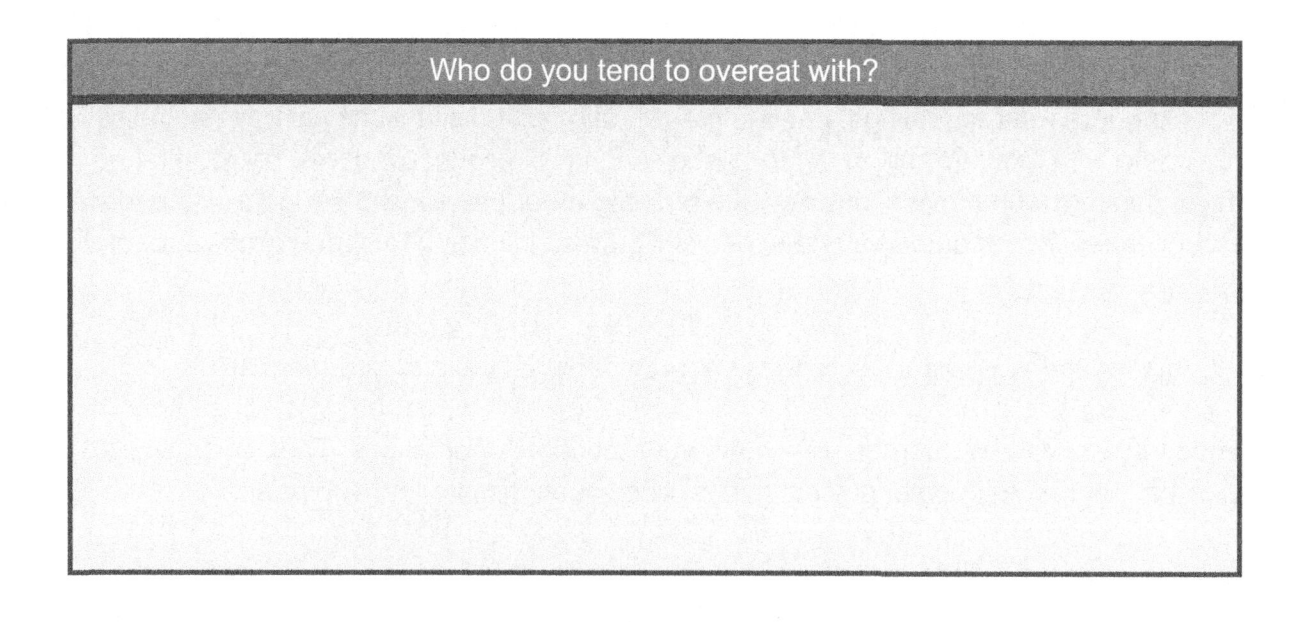

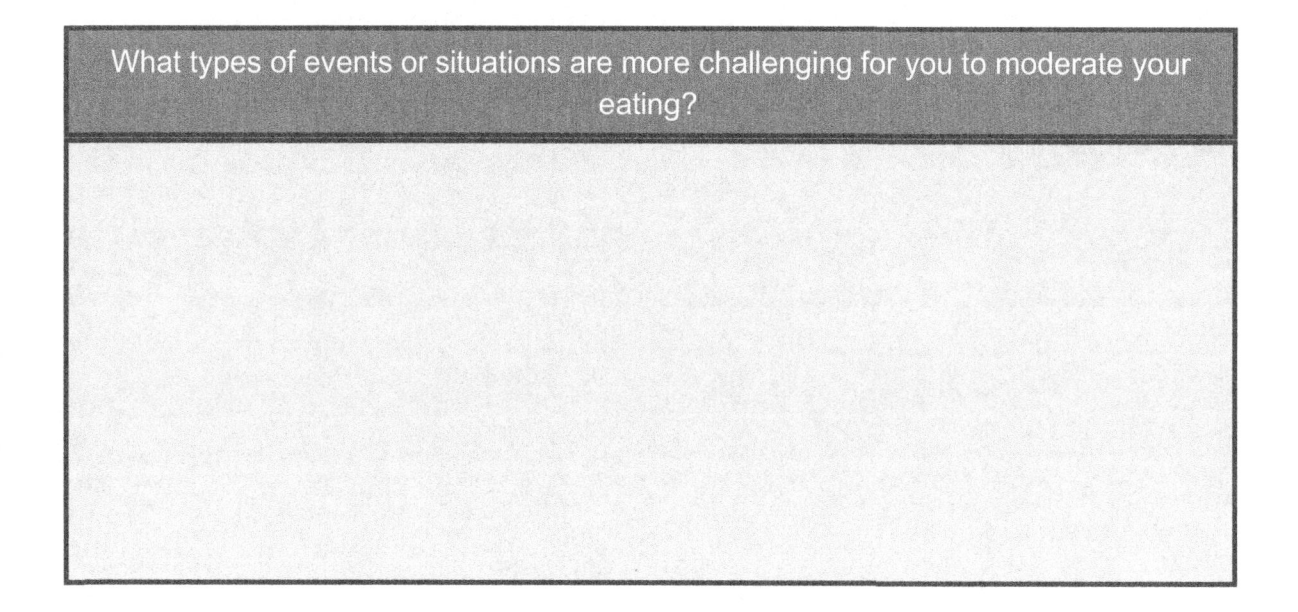

What types of events or situations are more challenging for you to moderate your eating?

In the early stages of making a change, it may be wise to consider limiting your exposure to certain triggers. Some external triggers like people you tended to overeat with, places where you tended to overeat, or certain foods which often lead to overeating can sometimes be avoided altogether in the early stages, which will help to make your change process easier.

Other triggers are not avoidable. Things like family get-togethers, catered work meetings, or even going to the grocery store can be major unavoidable triggers that people struggle with.

PLANNING AHEAD

Use this worksheet to write out upcoming situations where you would encounter unavoidable triggers. Use the space beneath to make a plan of what you will do in each situation.

Situation: Catered work party	**Situation:**
Specific Triggers: Good food that is free, unlimited drinks, snack options	**Specific Triggers:**
Plan: Small snack before party, ask wife to get food for me instead of getting it myself, limit to one plate of food	**Plan:**
Skills to overcome impulses: Pause and think it through, step outside for some air, reminding myself of how far I've come	**Skills to overcome impulses:**
Situation:	**Situation:**
Specific Triggers:	**Specific Triggers:**
Plan:	**Plan:**
Skills to overcome impulses:	**Skills to overcome impulses:**

FOOD DIARY

Grocery List (BEAT THE BINGE)

Food/Day	Monday	Tuesday	Wednesday	Thursday	Friday	Saturday	Sunday
Breakfast							
Drink							
Snack							
Lunch							
Drink							
Snack							
Dinner							
Drink							
Snack							

What we would like you to try is to find a better way of responding to your triggers. It's similar to pressing pause on your TV. Try this proven formula to help you to respond to your triggers in a healthier way...

#1. Think before you act: before you say yes or no, reach for second helpings, or buy food, take a few moments to weigh up the decision.

#2. Plan ahead: in situations where you know you will encounter triggers, plan ahead about how you will make good decisions in the moment. If you are going out to eat with friends, view the menu online and choose what you will order. If going to the grocery store, make a list and stick to it.

#3. Think of long-term reward: remind yourself of the long-term rewards associated with making healthy decisions. These might include feeling more in control, reaching a 30-day goal, or feeling less tired and drained.

#4. Remind yourself that you are in control and have a choice about whether to feed or starve the impulse. Consider consequences: think about the negative feelings you might experience afterwards like being uncomfortable or feeling guilty after overeating.

Pressing Pause on a Hunger Urge

When we experience a hunger urge, it's important to pause and think carefully about how we respond to it. Thinking carefully often means we need to 'slow down' our response time in order to respond in the best way.

Try to imagine that just like a video, you can slow down your actions in real-time. Pressing 'pause' gives you time to fully consider your options, rewinding to times when you have made this decision in the past, and fast-forwarding to consider the long-term rewards and consequences. If the decision has the potential to cause problems, you can press 'stop' to make a different decision, and 'play' when ready to act.

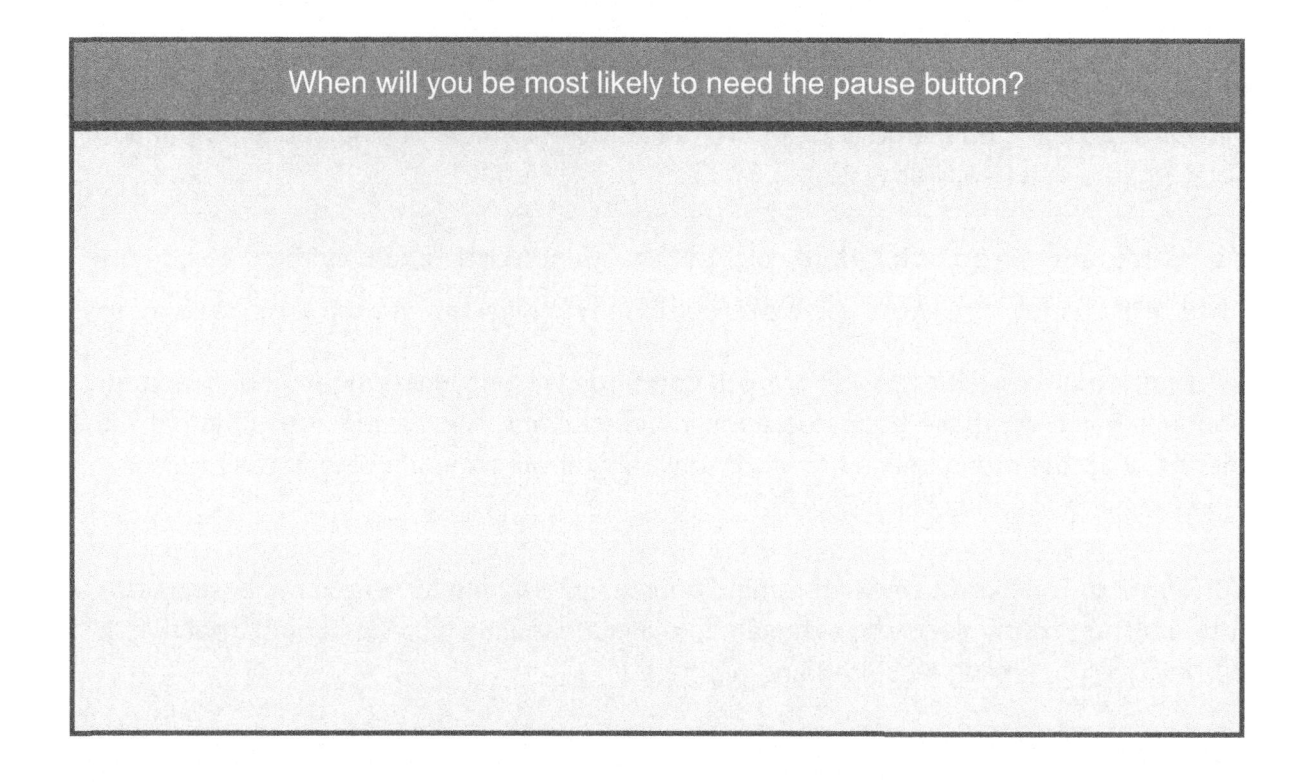

When will you be most likely to need the pause button?

This will certainly be challenging to do, as we have often developed patterns of behaviour around our overeating that will need to change. The more you practice thinking long term and making decisions based on your long-term goals, the easier it will become.

Now that you are more aware of the old associations you had with food that often cause these urges, what are the new associations you want to create?

Example: If the old association was between food and comfort, maybe the new association would be food as a way to maintain health. Or if the old association was between food and pleasure, the new association may be that food represents sustenance or energy your body needs.

When you press 'pause' in these situations, what long-term consequences and rewards can you consider that will help you make the best decision? These reminders can be an important part of helping to make daily choices that will reinforce the new connections and associations we are working to develop.

Are you Reacting or Responding?

Most actions and decisions we make are in reaction or response to an internal or external situation - a feeling or thought we have, or a request or situation that occurs. The difference between reaction and response is subtle but important to understand.
A reaction happens quickly, is often based on our immediate emotional response, is unplanned, and focused on what we want right now rather than our long-term needs. Examples of reacting include yelling and honking our horn at a driver, saying yes or no without thinking about the outcome, or making any snap decision that might cause problems later on.

A response, on the other hand, is more well thought-out. We have taken the time to assess the situation, evaluate our options, think through the potential consequences, and make a decision. Learning to 'pause' gives us time to slow our decision-making process down long enough to 'respond' rather than 'react'.

Thinking long-term

When we talk about making lasting changes, it is important to know the role that values, or guiding principles, have to play. Values represent the principles that are most important to who we are, how we behave, and what we want and need to have a full and meaningful life.

Values are related to goals but also different in important ways. Values are more about the process than the destination and are what motivates us to take action. For example, losing 10 pounds would be a goal, but the value behind it may be the importance of our health. Another example would be having a goal of wanting to be on time to work, but the value behind this may be related to wanting to be trustworthy or reliable.

Take a moment to think about your values in life

It is easier for you to reach your goals if they align with your values. What is important for you? You can't tell me that your health is important for you if you never exercise and you eat burgers and chips for breakfast, lunch, and dinner.

But let's say health is important for you and that you have not been looking after yourself well. Perhaps you have some other reasons why you have not been able to exercise and eat better. But if you know that from today you want to act in a way that everyone you meet will know that you value your health ask yourself...

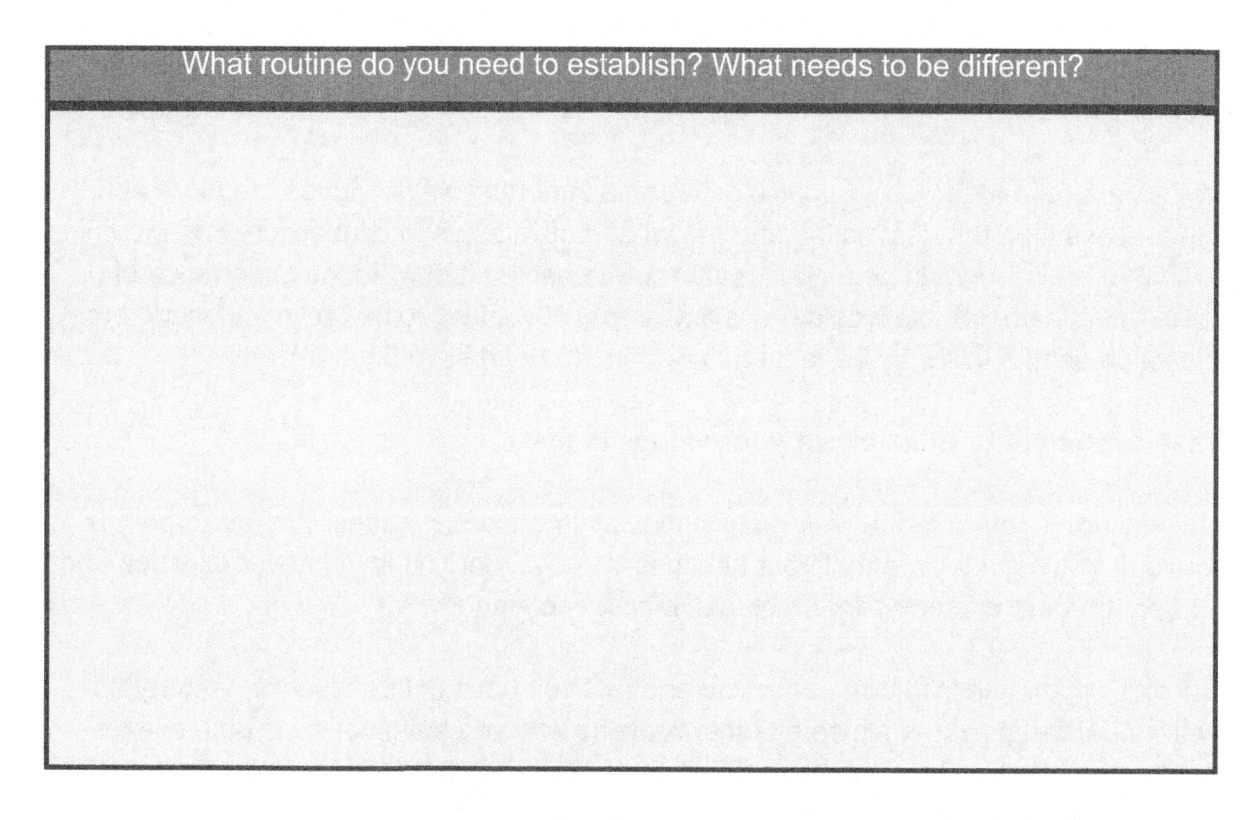

What do you need to change?

What routine do you need to establish? What needs to be different?

PERSONAL VALUES

Use the table below to select up to 5 values which represent your answers. Use the blank spaces at the bottom to write in any values not listed.

> What 5 ingredients would be needed for a meaningful life?
> What do you need in relationships in order to feel close to someone?
> During times when you've been most unhappy, what has been missing?
> What would the person closest to you say are your best qualities?
> What principles have guided major life decisions?

Adventure	Contribution	Friendship	Integrity	Originality	Status
Authority	Collaboration	Fun	Independence	Openness	Self-respect
Achievement	Courage	Fortune	Influence	Optimism	Trust
Accountability	Connection	Generosity	Insight	Peace	Vulnerability
Awareness	Curiosity	Growth	Justice	Productivity	Wisdom
Authenticity	Challenge	Grace	Kindness	Popularity	Wealth
Autonomy	Composure	Gentleness	Knowledge	Recognition	
Beauty	Determination	Hope	Logic	Respect	
Bravery	Dedication	Happiness	Leadership	Restraint	
Balance	Discipline	Honesty	Love	Responsibility	
Boldness	Education	Hardwork	Learning	Security	
Consistency	Equality	Humour	Loyalty	Stability	
Confidence	Fairness	Harmony	Meaning	Service	
Compassion	Faith	Helping	Mastery	Spirituality	
Creativity	Fame	Humility	Mindfulness	Success	

Next, use the space below to write in what behaviours or actions DEMONSTRATE these values and which behaviours or actions CONFLICT with these values:

DEMONSTRATING ACTIONS	CONFLICTING ACTIONS

After identifying your core values, consider which ones are related to changing your eating habits. Perhaps one of your core values is health. When making decisions, you can ask yourself if this action would move you further away from this value or closer to this value. Generally, decisions that move us towards our core values tend to be decisions we feel best about later on.

This is because values provide a guideline for being our best self and living our best life. When our actions are moving us closer towards our values, they are strengthened and when our actions are moving away from our values, our values are weakened.

> **"People often say that motivation doesn't last. Well, neither does bathing - that's why we recommend it daily."**
> ~ Zig Ziglar ~

Make a list of actions that move you towards and away from each of your core values and use this method as a way to help you evaluate your actions and make decisions that will move you closer to your best life, and best self.

Part 3 - HOW to Overcome Impulsive Overeating

"We are what we repeatedly do. Excellence, then, is not an act, but a habit."
~ Aristotle ~

Strategies & Tips for Addressing Overeating

Because overeating is such a common issue, there are strategies and tips you can learn to overcome it. These are things that have been proven to be effective with other people who have the same problem. The good news is that it is possible to interrupt the cycle of overeating and regain control over your eating habits, thereby improving your physical and mental health along the way. In this section you will learn tips and strategies that will help you to make a strong start on the path towards controlling your eating.

Difficult feelings: shame, guilt, and a lack of control.

Because of the stigma and shame associated with being overweight, many people try to hide their eating habits and even become closet overeaters. The more isolated and ashamed people feel, the less likely they are to reach out for help with this problem, and the less confident they will feel in their ability to overcome it. This can lead to avoiding any thoughts about the problem, going deeper into denial, and making excuses in order to continue the behaviour, thereby putting off the difficult task of making serious life changes. If you have struggled with conflicting feelings about making a lifestyle change, know that you are not alone.

Change can feel difficult, overwhelming, and even scary. It's normal to have part of you that doesn't want to change your eating habits but reading this book means that there is also a part of you that does.

That part of you might be worried about your health - maybe you have already noticed adverse effects due to your eating habits or weight. It might be harder to breathe, you may get winded or tired more easily, or you've just noticed that you are more tired, drained, or unfocused.

That part of you might be worried about your emotional and mental health - maybe you struggle with feelings of depression, shame, or low self-esteem. Maybe you have become highly self-critical, and have begun to spiral into patterns of moodiness, or sadness, or have become more irritable with others.

Or perhaps that part of you might be worried about your social life and relationships. Maybe you notice that people who you care about are making comments that are hurtful, and these change the way you feel about yourself or about them. Maybe you avoid certain social interactions or settings because you fear being judged by others for your weight or eating, and this can lead to feeling isolated and lonely.

Take a moment to reflect on your emotions and feelings:

How has overeating affected you?

What is the most challenging feeling for you?

What do you want to feel about yourself?

Whatever brought you to the point where you bought this book or signed up for this course, it is important to ask yourself these questions as you start this journey:

Why now? What has happened or changed, that makes this change necessary now?

What can I do to feel more confident in my ability to make this change and to make it last?

What will change about me, my life, and my future if I am able to make a lasting change to my eating habits?

Take a few moments to write these questions down and reflect on them, as they are integral to your success as you move through this program. There will be days when change seems not as important, too hard, or not worth it. Use the answers to these three questions to remind yourself of your long-term goals on these harder days.

Stop using scales

While losing weight is often a benefit of learning to control your eating, it should not be your main focus and only motivation.

One reason this is important, is because it is possible that after a few days or even a few weeks of eating healthily and moderating portions, it may not be reflected on the scales. Weight loss is a complex process impacted by several factors like health conditions and your metabolism. If your only motivation is to lose weight, you may become discouraged and feel like the changes you are making are not 'worth it' - especially if weight loss is not happening as quickly or easily as you expected.

Instead, if your focus is more on how you feel (i.e. how much energy you have, how you feel about yourself, and how in control of your choices you feel), then you are more likely to notice the other advantages and benefits of continuing to work on overeating. Don't make the scales the only way you measure your progress.

Write down what you will focus on and how you will measure your progress

Focus on positive and sustainable change

Another reason why it is important not just to focus on weight loss, is because research on dieting shows that sometimes restrictive dieting can actually lead to weight gain and long-term health problems.

Sometimes referred to as 'yo-yo dieting', this pattern of going on very restrictive diets is detrimental because they are often not sustainable over time. Research shows that making reasonable, gradual changes that you can stick with in the long term (also called lifestyle changes), is a much healthier and more effective way to manage your eating and your weight, over the course of a lifetime.

In the beginning, it may be wise or even necessary to cut out certain foods altogether as you start making lifestyle changes, but always remember to think about what changes you feel like you could commit to over a long term, and work to reintroduce or reincorporate moderate amounts of the foods you cut out as you start to feel more in control.

To make my journey sustainable and positive I will:

Avoid extremes

Finding a healthy balance is another essential part of breaking the cycle of overeating. Often, feelings of guilt and shame motivate people in the opposite direction, creating risks for undereating and malnutrition, overly restrictive diets, or excessive fitness routines, that can have just as detrimental an effect as overeating or under-exercising. Finding a healthy balance means being aware of the middle ground and working to establish healthy routines that help you maintain your health over the course of a lifetime.

Remind yourself of the importance of 'moderation' to avoid going to either extreme.

What is my middle ground? What is realistic and helpful for me to do in my first weeks of tackling impulsive overeating?

Write down your week 1–3 activities and changes that you would like to do:

In order to continue improving, for the next three weeks I will focus on… (Would you like to increase the time you spend exercising? Perhaps you would like to add a yoga class or hiking to make it more interesting and exciting for you?)

How can I maintain my new lifestyle to ensure that my nutrition is good, and that I get enough physical activity in my life on a regular basis?

You don't have to do it alone.

Finally, although it can be hard, involving people who care about us is an essential part of making a successful change. This is because people are social, and each individual is a part of much larger social systems that include family, friends, co-workers, and community members.

Food is frequently an important part of these social and cultural groups - think about how often a friend or co-worker asks you to join them for lunch, or how often there is food at family gatherings or other community gatherings that you are a part of. Letting certain people know that we are making changes to our eating can be important in helping them understand how they can best support us.
This is especially important for the people we are closest to and interact with the most. For example, if you have a significant other who you live with, letting them know that you are working to change your eating habits is important, because you will probably need to make changes that will affect what types of food you buy at the grocery store, or what kinds of meals are planned for the week.

More tips to plan well

#1 - If you want organic and more affordable fruits and vegetables, try local fresh produce markets. In many suburbs, on weekends you can buy produce from local farmers.

#2 - Buy fruits and veggies that are in season, they are obviously going to be much cheaper. If you have the time and space in your garden, start growing easy plants like herbs and tomatoes that will eventually save you money and a trip to the shop.

#3 - Do research online to find great recipes and then experiment with them on weekends.

#4 - Prepare your healthy weekday lunches in advance.

#5 - If you hate cooking and preparing meals, do research on what other options are available to you. It doesn't have to be your traditional calorie-restricted meals – many different artisan options are available to dieters now.

#6 - If you cannot bring your own lunch to work, research your local takeaway shops, there is always a healthier option for you to select.

#7 - Do small swaps. For example, even if you are choosing your local Thai takeaway, swap your usual coke for water, or swap deep-fried spring rolls for a small salad.

#8 - Even if you feel that you didn't make the best choice for lunch, don't give up today, just plan for a better dinner.

#9 - If you didn't plan well and now you are standing in a store staring at that rather expensive avocado and want to throw the whole health-food quest out of the window, simply pause and look around. What other options are available to you? What other vegetables or fruits can you purchase? What else will be both nutritious and make you feel good after eating it?

Cognitive Behavioural Therapy

Learning to recognise your own cognitive distortions will help you ignore a negative thought or actively change it. Recognising and changing your cognitive distortions will help you change the way you feel and the way you behave.

Cognitive distortions are misperceptions and misinterpretations about what is really happening. These misinterpretations are thoughts that come to our mind automatically. They can affect the way we think and act. For this reason, they are called "negative automatic thoughts" (NATs).

Have you ever looked at a pen placed in a glass full of water? If you do this, you'll see that the pen looks broken! So, sometimes our thoughts are a distorted version of reality.
In this part of the program, you will learn about the most common cognitive distortions.

Please take your time and go through each cognitive distortion very carefully and think about the type of cognitive distortion(s) you might have.

People normally have these thinking errors, but sometimes they can be so intense they affect our feelings and behaviour in a negative way.

Let's take a look at how cognitive behavioural therapy (CBT) helps in managing your urges and impulses…

CBT is structured and goal oriented with the main goal of helping you to…

#1 - Identify your negative automatic thoughts (or cognitive distortions) as discussed in the previous sessions
#2 - Learn some ways to modify these unhelpful thinking patterns
#3 - Unlearn your unwanted reactions that lead to unhelpful impulsive behaviour

For example, a person who has problems with binge eating might have these recurrent thoughts: "I am going to get full eventually, I might as well just keep eating until I can't manage any more…"

Some of the cognitive distortions that you might experience are:

Cognitive Distortion Types

1. Instant Satisfaction

I have a right to immediate satisfaction, without waiting or working. Life should be easy. Examples of negative automatic thoughts: "I need it now." "I have to do what I feel like doing."

2. Shoulds

There are rules about how the world should work. When the rules are violated, I feel angry. Examples: "No one should criticize me." "It should be easy to find a job."

3. Fooling Yourself

I sometimes trick myself into believing that something is OK when it is not. Example: "My ex-boyfriend may have abused me, but it'll be OK to call him just to say hello."

HALF A CUPCAKE IS NOT A CUPCAKE, IT DOES NOT COUNT.

4. Overreacting

I make a mountain out of a molehill. Things take on "life or death" proportions in my mind, beyond what is rational. Examples: "I'll never get over the fact that he (she) left me." "I'll die if I don't get that job."

MY LIFE IS OVER… I MIGHT AS WELL BE DEAD.
DARLING, WHAT HAPPENED?
OUR INTERNET IS DOWN…

5. Jumping to Conclusions

I draw conclusions in the absence of evidence to support the conclusion or when the evidence is contrary to the conclusion. Examples: "If I go to that party, no one will like me." "I am going to be sacked (or fail my exams)."

6. Fortune Telling

I think I know what the future will bring, and I expect disaster and gloom. Example: "I'll never have friends who truly care about me."

7. Confusing Needs and Wants

I want something very badly, so I think I have to have it. Example: "I have to have it."

8. Focusing on the Negatives and Discounting Positives

I magnify all the negatives in a situation, and ignore all the positives. Examples: "I said something stupid, and now I feel like an idiot." "I cannot do anything right." I claim that the positive things I or others do are trivial. Example: "Those successes were easy, so they don't matter."

9. All or Nothing Thinking

Things are black or white, good or bad. I have to be perfect or I am a failure. There is no middle ground. Examples: "I get rejected by everyone." "It was a complete waste of time."

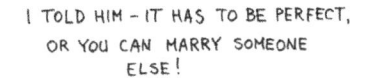

10. Catastrophising

I believe that what has happened, or will happen, will be so awful and unbearable that I won't be able to stand it. Example: "It would be terrible if I failed."

11. Overgeneralizing

I perceive a global pattern of negatives on the basis of a single incident. Example: "This generally happens to me. I seem to fail at a lot of things."

12. Personalising

I attribute a disproportionate amount of the blame for negative events to myself, and I fail to see that certain events are also caused by others. Examples: "The relationship (marriage) ended because I failed." "It was all my fault."

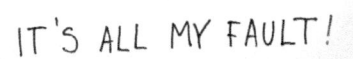

13. Regret Orientation

I focus on the idea that I could have done better in the past rather than paying attention to what I could do better now. Example: "I shouldn't have said that."

14. Short-Term Thinking

Like a horse with blinders on, I see only what's directly in front of me. I focus only on the short term (how I'll feel in a few minutes) rather than the long term (how I'll feel in a few hours, or tomorrow, or later in life). Example: "I'll just do it; nothing I try makes any difference."

15. Emotional Reasoning

I let my feelings guide my interpretation of reality. Example: "I feel guilty so I must have done something wrong."

16. Labelling

I assign global negative traits to myself and others. Examples: "I'm undesirable." or "He is a nasty person."

17. Negative Filtering

I almost always focus on the negatives and seldom notice the positives. Example: "Look at all of the people who don't like me."

Imagine you have an urge to do something quickly without thinking about its consequences, then write your answers in the table below:

- When I have an urge or impulse to do…
- My negative thought is…
- My negative distortion is…

Here are some examples to illustrate how it works…

- When I have an urge or impulse to… eat another slice of cake
- My negative thought is…who cares I will go for a run later
- My negative distortion is…fooling myself
- When I have an urge or impulse to…go to drive through on the way home to have a dinner
- My negative thought is…I am fat, I will never get better, who cares, I am a failure
- My negative distortion is…catastrophizing

Were you surprised that there were so many types of cognitive distortions?

Now, please take your time and think about the following questions and incomplete sentences.

> 1. Have you experienced any of these thinking errors before or while you were engaging in unhelpful impulsive behaviour?

2. Which one (if any) do you think you may have in your mind when you experience an urge or impulse?

My thinking error(s) might be...

1. Instant satisfaction
2. Shoulds
3. Fooling yourself
4. Overreacting
5. Jumping to conclusions
6. Fortune telling
7. Confusing needs and wants
8. Focusing on the negatives and discounting the positives
9. All or nothing thinking
10. Catastrophising
11. Overgeneralising
12. Personalising
13. Regret orientation
14. Short-term thinking
15. Emotional reasoning
16. Labelling
17. Negative filtering

Disputing my impulsive thoughts...		
So what is the alternate explanation?	How does thinking in this way make me feel?	How does this affect my urge or desire to act?

Let's take a look at our next formula to see if your arguments for having these thoughts are accurate…

When I think the following...
What evidence do I have which supports my thoughts?
What evidence do I have that does not support my thoughts?

When I think the following... I just want to have another burger, I feel hungry I have to have it, I am starving.

What evidence do I have which supports my thoughts? I feel hunger, I want to eat.

What evidence do I have that does not support my thoughts? I had a good breakfast and I had a snack an hour ago.

When I think the following... I just want to eat that cake, who cares, I am just going to be fat.

What evidence do I have which supports my thoughts? I failed at good eating habits in the past, I always end up here.

Every time we try to break an old habit and replace it with a new one we must expect it to take time. At the beginning there will be occasions when you will suddenly find yourself in the middle of the familiar unwanted situation. Try not to act on the spur of the moment. Pull back from the situation. Take a wider view; compose yourself.

Use 'STOPP' to deal with this situation - STOP-THINK-ACT

STOPP-THINK-ACT

S - STOPP AND STEP BACK
T - TAKE A BREATH
O - OBSERVE, THINK
P - PULL BACK
P - PRACTICE WHAT WORKS

STOPP Method CBT in a Nutshell by:
getselfhelp.co.uk

Step 1: Stop and step back (from the situation, in your mind). Don't act immediately or automatically. Pause.

Step 2: Take a breath. Notice your breath as you breathe in and out.

Step 3: Observe or ask yourself "what am I thinking and feeling?". What are the words that my mind is saying? Are the thoughts: accurate or inaccurate? Helpful or unhelpful? Is this thought, fact or opinion? Where is my focus of attention?

Step 4: Pull back. See the situation as an outside observer. What would a fly on the wall see? Is there another way of looking at it? What would someone else see and make of it? What advice would I give to someone else in this situation? What meaning am I giving this event that is making me react in this way? How important is it right now, and will it be in 6 months? Is my reaction in proportion to the event?

Step 5: Practise what works. Do what works and what helps! Play to your principles and values. Will it be effective and appropriate? Is it in proportion to the event? Is it in keeping with my values and principles? What will be the consequences of my action? What is best for me and most helpful in this situation?

Now can you examine your negative automatic thoughts? Try the following: imagine you have an urge to do something quickly without thinking about its consequences, then write your answers below:

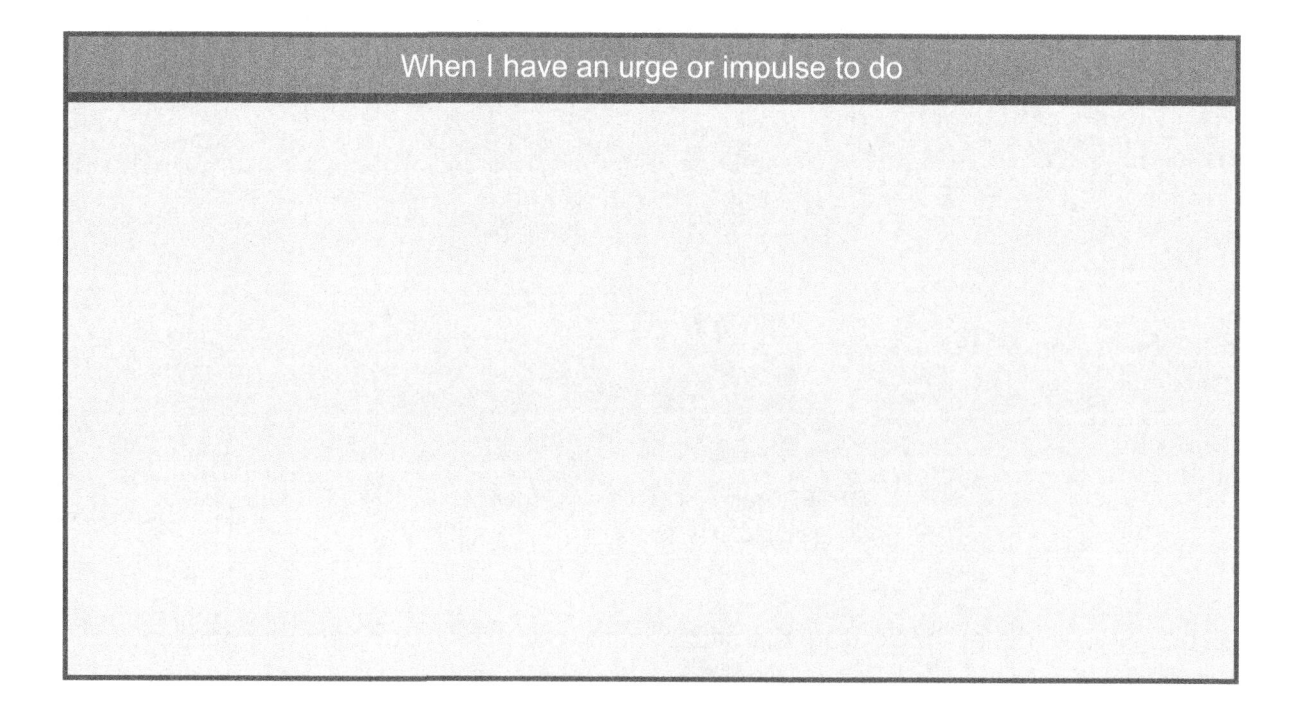

When I have an urge or impulse to do

My negative thought is

My negative distortion is

IDENTIFYING MY NEGATIVE COGNITIVE DISTORTIONS

Urge or Impulse	Negative Thought	Cognitive Distortion
"I have to have a glass of wine."	*"It always happens to me. I never get what I want."*	Overgeneralization

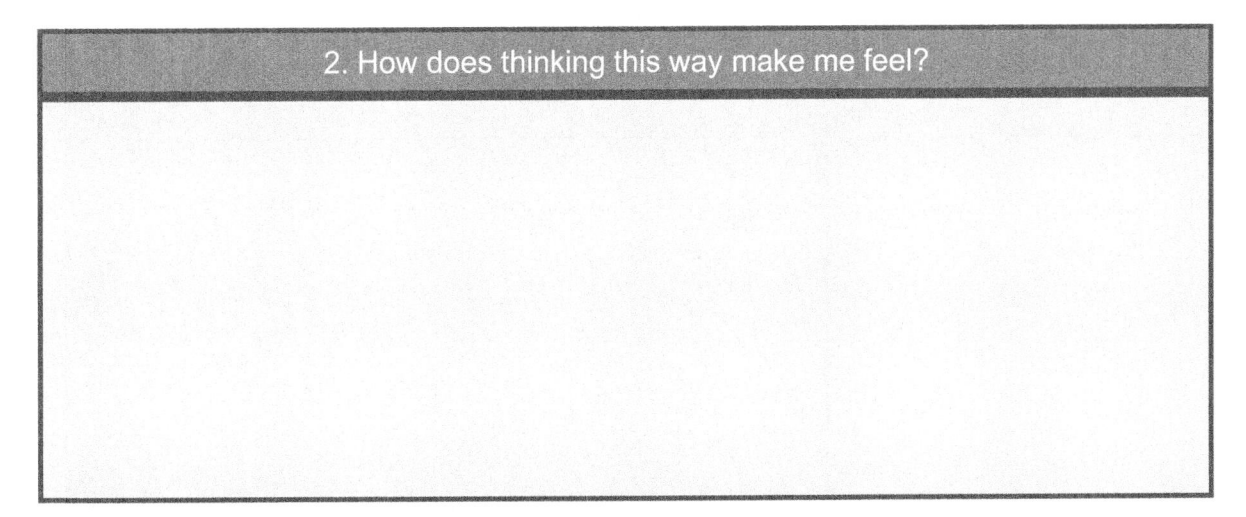

Now… let's dispute the impulsive thoughts. The process will be complete once you answer the following questions:

1. What's an alternate explanation?

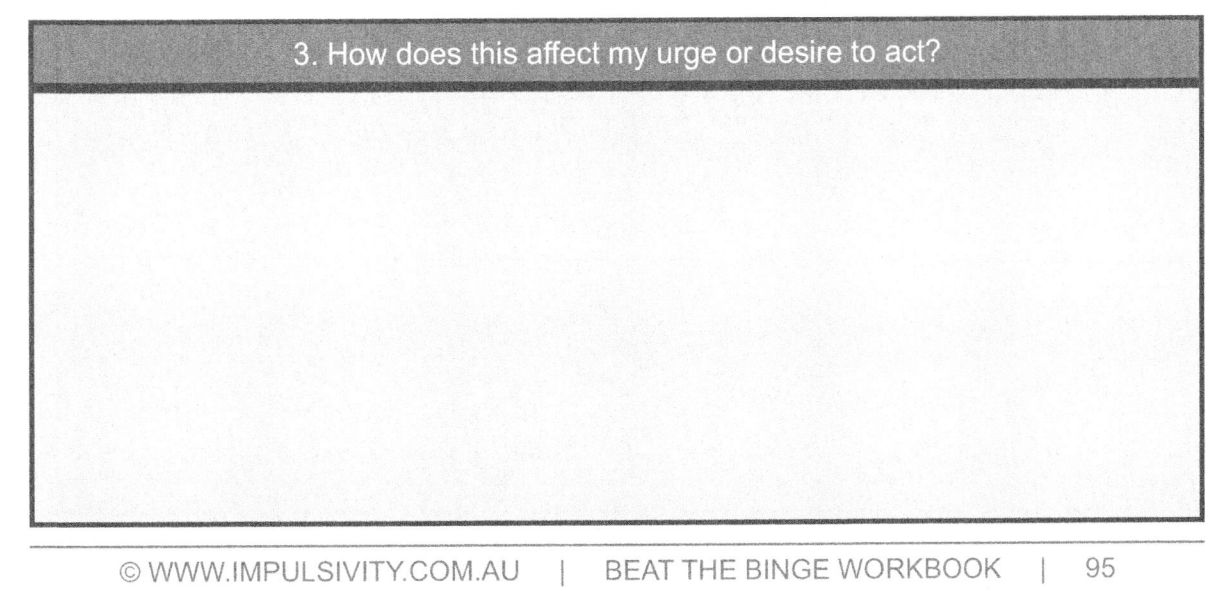

2. How does thinking this way make me feel?

3. How does this affect my urge or desire to act?

DISPUTING MY IMPULSIVE THOUGHTS

1. What is an alternate explanation?	2. How does thinking this way make me feel?	3. How does this affect my urge or desire to act?

I have identified my cognitive distortion, it is _____.

I know how to identify my cognitive distortions. First, I ask myself: "When I have an urge to do something, what is my negative automatic thought?" Firstly, I pay attention to the negative automatic thoughts and then I can identify my cognitive distortion.

Now I know that it is not helpful to think this way and I have learnt a way to dispute old cognitive distortions:

When I think the following:

What evidence do I have that supports my thoughts?

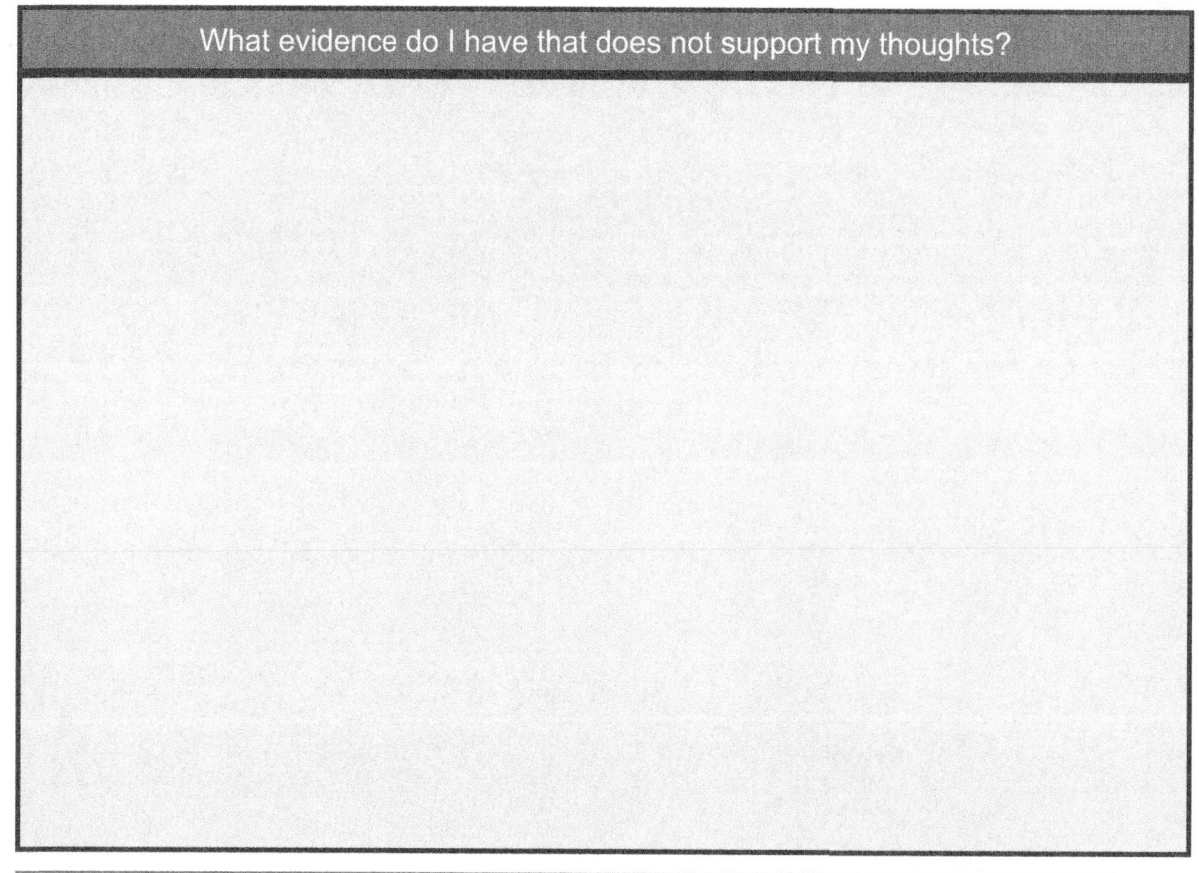

What evidence do I have that does not support my thoughts?

Develop & Protect your New Mindset

Working to establish any sort of new routine or habit starts with our mindset. We all have a number of unhelpful beliefs which are sometimes called cognitive distortions.

Cognitive distortions are simply ways that our mind convinces us of something that isn't really true. Some common inaccurate thoughts that lead to overeating include;

- Minimization (at least I didn't have a refill)
- Justification (excuses like: I've been good on my diet all week so it's ok to cheat now…)
- Comparison (at least I didn't eat as much as my friend)
- Blame (if my spouse didn't buy chips, I wouldn't have overeaten)
- Emotional reasoning (I was just stressed, that's why I overate).

Watch out for these thoughts, because they often are the first sign of a bad decision!

Change is necessary
It is possible for me to change
Changing my eating habits is worth it

Inner Critic

We all have an inner critic and it is no surprise that we are often harder on ourselves than on anyone else. This inner critic needs to be supervised as we start our change process, as it can quickly get us off track.

Our inner critic lives in a part of our mind that could be called the 'problem solving' mind - or the part of our mind that works to identify problems and generate solutions. This means that our critic can actually be helpful, but often does not know the best way to help and resorts to harsh methods of pointing out flaws and mistakes.

> **"Feeling sorry for yourself, and your present condition, is not only a waste of energy, but the worst habit you can possibly have."**
>
> ~ Dale Carnegie ~

Sometimes, we can ask our critic to work in more helpful ways. If you find that your critic is pointing out all of the mistakes you have made, try asking it to think about how you can avoid these mistakes in the future. In general, keeping your critic focused on the solution instead of the problem is a good way to teach it how to be more helpful.

Monitor, Track & Be Accountable

Pay closer attention to what, when, and how much you are eating. Part of this includes using a mindful approach to eating - paying attention to your behaviour in the moment. Not in a judging way, but in a way where you are being honest and accountable with yourself about what you put into your body.

Because much of overeating is based on impulsivity (or not thinking all the way through our choices), paying closer attention is an essential first step. Many people find that having some sort of a system, like an app that counts your calories, a list of what you will eat for the day, or keeping a food diary are helpful tools, especially in the early phases of change.

- Food diary
- Mobile app
- Fitbit

How can I be accountable for my behaviour? How can I record everything that I consume accurately?

> "In essence, if we want to direct our lives, we must take control of our consistent actions. It's not what we do once in a while that shapes our lives, but what we do consistently."
>
> ~ Tony Robbins ~

Self-Care and Self-Compassion

Developing a new relationship with food often means developing a new relationship with ourselves - learning to treat ourselves and our bodies with respect, kindness, and compassion.

Self-compassion promotes resilience. It helps with emotional regulation, taking actions (including setting goals), and helps to reduce stress. When we experience diet transgression and we are extremely critical, we are more likely to give up. But if we show a bit of self-compassion – saying, ok everyone makes mistakes and if we are a bit more realistic, such self-compassion facilitates goal persistence.

And research shows that it will take us couple of times to try and go through a process of change until we get it completely right. We highly recommend checking out Dr Kristin Neff who dedicated decades studying self-compassion.

In the early stages of making a change, we may need to have more structures in place and more rigid guidelines to help us stay on track with our goals.

But as you experience success, you will learn to trust yourself more to make healthy and respectful decisions for yourself and your body, and some of these guidelines can become a little more flexible.

Many people who struggle with overeating also struggle with negative feelings about their weight, appearance, and body. This can be a major issue as you work to develop healthier lifestyle habits, because if you hate your body, then you are less likely to treat it in ways that are respectful.

If thinking about loving your body is difficult, start small by thinking about specific parts of your body that you like, or by thinking of times when you feel most comfortable and confident in your body.

This could be when you are intimate with your significant other, when you are dressed nicely for a special occasion, or when you are using your body to exercise or play a sport that you love. Next, work up from there by trying to think of one new thing or activity related to your body that you appreciate every single day. Like all new behaviours, the more you practice this, the easier it will become.

Many people put 'conditions' on whether they love and accept themselves. These conditions can be related to external measures of success, like: "I'm only good enough if I have this kind of job" or "if I make this amount of money". These conditions can also be related to our appearance or size, like: "I'm only good enough if I am under this weight" or "can fit into this size".

> **Take a close, honest look at ways that you have made self-acceptance or self-love conditional… what are these conditions?**

How have they made you feel when you didn't meet them?

How are they holding you back from being your best self and living your best life?

SELF-CRITICISM VS SELF-COMPASSION

Use a recent mistake you made to think of both a self-critical way of thinking about the mistake (i.e.: blaming yourself or thinking "I'm so stupid!", etc.) and a self-compassionate way of thinking about the mistake (i.e.: realizing you are only human or thinking "I can still make this right" or "I can learn from this") and then fill out the remaining spaces to explore the impact of each type of thought.

SPECIFIC SKILL	BENEFIT/USE
Critical thoughts after making a mistake:	Kind thoughts after making a mistake:
How these thoughts affect my mood:	How these thoughts affect my mood:
How these thoughts affect my self-esteem:	How these thoughts affect my self-esteem:
How these thoughts affect my motivation:	How these thoughts affect my motivation:
What behaviour/choices these thoughts lead to:	What behaviour/choices these thoughts lead to:
The likely consequences of these choices:	The likely consequences of these choices:

SELF COMPASSION LETTER

Use this worksheet as a template to write a self-compassion letter that focuses on being compassionate, kind, forgiving, and positive about the way your body looks and feels.

DEAR _____

I know you have struggled with feeling as though your body is: _____
_____

and that it's really difficult not to blame yourself because you have mistreated your body in these ways:
_____

You can forgive yourself for this because you have been treating your body better by making these changes: _____
_____

It's really making a positive difference in: _____
_____

On days that you mess up, I want to remind you that you are: _____
_____

that I am proud of you for: _____
_____

and that I know you are capable of: _____
_____

On days that are just really hard, keep in mind: _____
_____

and that doing these things usually help: _____
_____

and that if they don't, you can always call on these people for support: _____
_____

Don't give up on yourself, because making these changes will help you: _____
_____
_____

P.S. _____
_____

If you find that there are conditions you have placed on whether you love and accept yourself, it is important to work on developing a new relationship with yourself that does not have conditions. While you may still feel upset or disappointed in yourself at times, you will be able to put these mistakes in perspective and be better able to move on from them in a healthy way.

Mindfulness

Mindfulness is a skill - first it needs to be learned and practiced so it can help you deal with difficult feelings. Mindfulness means paying attention in a particular way:

on purpose,
in the present moment,
and non-judgmentally.

You don't have to do anything. You don't have to react or be overwhelmed by sensations. You simply observe, notice, and let go of any sensations and feelings.

Take a moment to reflect back on your life. Have there been times when you did not give in to an urge when it occurred?

Most of us have experienced urges passing. Maybe there were times when you felt the urge to go to your favourite take out or eat another slice of cake but waited long enough and then forgot about it.

It might feel strange at first. Usually, when we feel something unpleasant we try to make the situation better, so we don't have to feel this way anymore.

Mindfulness helps us to better understand our feelings and thoughts. Our thoughts and emotions are not facts.

If you think and feel that you are a bad person, it does not mean that you are one.

MY THOUGHTS AND EMOTIONS ARE NOT FACTS... THEY ARE JUST THOUGHTS AND EMOTIONS.

The more we practise mindfulness the more we learn that our thoughts are just thoughts. We learn not to react immediately but to stand back and observe them. In other words, you experience the changing nature and impermanence of urges.

> Take a moment now, close your eyes and imagine a time in which you felt the urge but did not engage in unhelpful impulsive behaviour. Describe that situation briefly below:

What does mindfulness look like when you practice? Let's give it a go. Let's start just with one-minute mindfulness exercise. Simply follow the instructions below.

1-Minute Mindfulness Exercise

1. Sit in a straight-backed chair, position your feet flat on the floor. Close your eyes or lower your gaze.

2. Focus your attention on your breath as it flows in and out. Don't try to change it in any way, just observe it without looking for anything special to happen.

3. After a while your mind may wander. When you notice this, gently bring your attention back to your breath, without giving yourself a hard time about it. Realising that your mind wanders without criticising yourself for it is central to the practice of mindfulness.

4. Just continue breathing. You may notice complete stillness - it may only be fleeting. If you notice any feelings - anger, exasperation, frustration - they may be fleeting too. Whatever happens, just allow it to be as it is.

5. After a minute, let your eyes slowly open.

Below is another meditation exercise that you might like to try. You can also search online for things like the 'train meditation' or 'urge surfing' until you find a technique that you prefer.

Imagine you are **the mountain – firm, grounded, present.**

Your thoughts are like the weather moving over you - the wind is blowing, and rain is pouring as streams of water form and rush down the mountain.

All the while the mountain remains unmoved, observing and being present amidst all the activity and storms of life and thoughts.

Some people admire mountain, others say it is not to their liking, but mountain remains the same. During sunny warm days and windy and rainy days mountain is the same it doesn't change it is firm and grounded and at peace.

MINDFULNESS PRACTICE LOG

Use the worksheet below to record your practice of mindfulness skills in each category, noting what skill you used (i.e.: grounding), the date and the situation (i.e.: after stressful day at work). Use the last column to note any benefits you noticed while using the skill or after, and identify when you think the skill would be the most helpful (i.e.: when trying to relax at night vs. starting the day).

MINDFULNESS PRACTICE	SPECIFIC SKILL	BENEFIT/USE
BODY-CENTERED PRACTICES Body Scan Breath Awareness Progressive Muscle Relaxation	Date/Situation: Skill:	Benefits Noticed:
	Date/Situation: Skill:	Times when these skills would be most useful:
ATTENTION TRAINING Single Tasking Guided Imagery	Date/Situation: Skill:	Benefits Noticed:
	Date/Situation: Skill:	Times when these skills would be most useful:
SENSORY PRACTICES Grounding 5 Senses	Date/Situation: Skill:	Benefits Noticed:
	Date/Situation: Skill:	Times when these skills would be most useful:

Nutrition Chapter

Nutrition can seem like a complex topic. There's a wealth of misinformation online with thousands of articles that promote conflicting evidence. One minute you're told something is a 'superfood' and the next it's thought to cause cancer. With so much confusion about nutrition, it can be easy to ignore everything and stick with what you know...

But there are some scientifically-sound principles that will make a big difference to your health. If you can learn a few fundamentals, then you'll be able to decide for yourself which information is worth listening to. If you struggle with impulsive binge eating, you'll also be able to adjust your habits and make more informed decisions relating to your impulses.

The Basics of Nutrition

Do you eat for fuel or pleasure? Although food can taste amazing, its primary purpose is to provide your body with energy. This energy is used for every single thing that you do, from breathing to thinking, and walking to dancing. It powers all the tiny reactions that allow your brain to function and muscles to move.

We usually describe food energy in terms of calories. Although they have negative connotations, they're really just a unit of measurement, like miles or minutes. We usually divide calories into three uses:

1. **Basic metabolic rate -** This is the number calories we need to minimally fuel the body e.g. thinking, breathing, sleeping. It hardly changes day to day and is influenced by things like our height and weight.
2. **Physical activity -** This is the number of calories we need to be active. It can vary greatly depending on what we do, such as sitting on the sofa watching TV versus running a marathon.
3. **Digestion -** This is the number of calories that are used in digesting food and usually account for 5-10% of our total calorie intake.

Calculating How Many Calories You Need

The number of calories you need to fuel your body will depend on many things. Your height, body mass, age, and activity levels can all influence how many calories you burn. Luckily, there's a handy formula that you can use to calculate your own needs…

Step 1 - Calculate your basic metabolic rate

Use the right formula for your gender and age-range below…

Gender & Age	Calculation
Female 18-30	15 x your weight in kg, then add 487
Male 18-30	15 x your weight in kg, then add 692
Female 30-60	8 x your weight in kg, then add 846
Male 30-60	11 x your weight in kg, then add 873
Female >60	9 x your weight in kg, then add 659
Male >60	12 x your weight in kg, then add 588

For example, a 30-year-old female who weighed 60kg would do the following…

$$(8 \times 60) + 846 = 1326 \text{ calories}$$

This is your basic metabolic rate, or the number of calories you need to fuel the fundamentals of life (before you do any moving).

Step 2 - Multiply this by your activity level

The next step is to multiply this by your level of activity. So, if you're fairly sedentary and work in an office all day then multiply your basic metabolic rate by 1.2. If you have a manual job and like to relax at night, then multiply it by 1.5. If you have an active job and run every evening, then multiply it by 1.7.

So, using the previous example, if this person was sedentary then their calculation would look like...

$$1326 \times 1.2 = 1591$$

The total number of calories this person would need to eat daily is 1591. This would ensure they don't gain weight or lose weight. Increasing or decreasing calorie intake either way could cause a weight change accordingly. So, now you know how to calculate exactly how many calories your body needs!

> *Activity* → *Follow the steps above to calculate how many calories you should really be consuming each day.*

Nutrients

Calories are just the start of good nutrition. The types of foods you consume also do different jobs within the body. Carbohydrate, fat, and protein are the building block of everything within our system. But for everything to work as it should, you need to consume each of these macronutrients in the right ratio.

Carbohydrate

- Carbohydrates are usually broken down into a sugar called glucose which is the primary fuel source for your brain and muscles.
- Rice, pasta, potatoes, cereal, bread, fruit, and vegetables are all good sources of carbohydrate.
- These should make up 40-50% of your calorie intake.

Fat

- Fats are broken down into smaller parts which are used to create cell membranes in every part of your body.
- Milk, cheese, butter, oils, nuts, and avocados are all good sources of fat.
- These should make up 20-30% of your calorie intake.

Protein

- Protein is broken down into amino acids which are used to create almost every other

structure in our body, including bone, hair, skin, and enzymes.
- Meat, fish, tofu, tempeh, beans, and pulses are all good sources of protein.
- These should make up around 20% of your calorie intake.

If you eat the right amount of each micronutrient then your body will function well. But if you have too much or too little, then you won't feel your best. What some people consider everyday symptoms like tiredness, bloating, and constipation, can be caused by an imbalance of nutrients.

Eating too much of anything can lead to weight gain. Most people think that fat makes you fat, but too much carbohydrate gets stored as excess energy too. Carbohydrate gets attached to water when it's stored, which makes it weight four times as much! And can make the scales seem even more depressing...

Micronutrients - Vitamins & Minerals

Many people eat plenty of calories but don't consume enough vitamins and minerals. In the western world, many people are considered 'malnourished' despite that fact that they eat three square meals a day. This is because they're getting enough energy to operate but not all the tiny nutrients that make the body function at its absolute best. These are things like iron, calcium, and vitamin C.

Vitamin and mineral deficiencies can lead to memory loss, inability to concentrate, skin conditions, and numerous other problems. They also help your body to break down carbohydrates, fats, and proteins, so they ensure you get the most out of your food. Likewise, they support the reactions involved in fat breakdown, so can stop you from seeing the weight loss results you want.

Fluids

The majority of your body is made up of water, so drinking enough fluids is essential to good health. Water supports all of the functions within your body yet few of us drink enough. Although we get some of our fluid intake from food (like fruit and vegetables) we should still aim to drink two litres a day. Water is best, but cordial, tea, and coffee also count. Fizzy drinks or fruit juices (even natural ones) should be consumed in moderation as they contain a lot of sugar. This can mean that we're drinking a lot more calories than we realise and lead to unexpected weight gain.

5 Practical Nutrition Strategies That You Can Try Today

There are lots of nutritional strategies that you can use to achieve your health goals. But this is part of the reason that healthy eating can be so overwhelming. So, we recommend starting with just one strategy until it becomes an everyday habit. Once it's second-nature, you can work on developing another habit and then another. Here are five effective starting strategies that you may like to try…

#1 - Focus on Fluids

Before you try to change your food habits, look at your fluids. The majority of us don't drink enough water, which not only keeps us hydrated but makes us feel fuller too. Not drinking enough fluids can make you feel tired which causes many of us to reach for sugary snacks as a boost. So, the first thing to do is ensure you're drinking 2 litres (around 6-8 glasses) a day.

If you're not used to drinking regularly then here are a few tips that can help…

- Carry a water bottle with you at all times and keep it on your work desk or study space
- Put visual prompts like post-it notes on your fridge or laptop screen to remind you to drink
- Commit to drinking a glass of water with every single meal or snack you consume

#2 - Get Your Greens

Instead of trying to cut out unhealthy foods cold-turkey, start by adding more good stuff. Don't try to restrict your intake of sweets or fast food right out of the gate. Begin by nourishing your body with more of the nutrient-rich foods that it's probably craving. Eating more vegetables (especially greens like broccoli, kale, and spinach) will address many vitamin and mineral deficiencies so you feel more energised throughout the day.

Once you're eating enough vegetables, you'll naturally eat less of the naughty stuff. This is because vegetables contain a lot of fibre which makes you feel full. So, there'll be less space for more food and you won't feel as hungry. They eventually displace the less healthy foods, until you begin to crave them to feel satisfied. Here are some easy ways to incorporate more greens into your diet;

- Add a handful of leafy greens into a fruit smoothie

- Make a vegetable-based omelette or mini-frittatas by pouring the mix into a cupcake tray
- Include a side salad with every meal you eat out - burgers, pasta dishes, everything.

#3 - Plan Ahead

If you eat impulsively, then you likely have a trigger that sets you off. It might be emotional, stress-related, or the physical feeling of hunger. If it's the latter, then a key strategy is to stop it before it starts. Don't let yourself get so hungry that you'll eat whatever is quick and easy (which usually ends up being junk food).

Ensure that you always have healthy food choices in the house. Along with all of the other CBT and mindfulness strategies outlined in this book, this will give you a fighting chance of making a good decision when temptation strikes. Ordering your food online can be an effective way to keep your cupboards stocked up with little effort. Save your shopping basket so you can repeat the same order on a weekly or fortnightly basis with one click. This also removes the temptations of attractive packaging and special offers that come with traipsing around a supermarket.

#4 - Brainstorm Healthy Substitutes

Let's be real here, very few of us are ever going to find 'kale chips' appetising. They're just not an equal substitute for salty, crunchy, shop-bought chips. They might look inspiring on Instagram but are unlikely to replace our trusty packaged snacks. But with a little trial and error, you might discover another healthy snack that you actually enjoy eating…

When we feel the urge for snacks, there's usually something that's driving it. What is the underlying reason that we want those chips? Are we craving comfort? Is it boredom? Genuine hunger? Now think about what it is that makes these chips so satisfying… is it that they're crunchy? Salty? Is it just the idea of treating ourselves as a reward for a hard day of work? Depending on what it is that you like about them, you can brainstorm healthier substitutes…

- Carrot sticks, cucumber batons, and apple wedges served with dip can satisfy hunger.
- Most chip manufacturers offer 'healthier' alternatives with less fat and salt but still satisfy the treat factor.
- Some types of cereal bar can satisfy a sweet tooth without the calories of chocolate and biscuits.

#5 - Batch Prepare

Batch preparing meals ensures that you always have a healthy option in the fridge or freezer. If you feel tempted to order fast food, knowing you have an alternative that's ready to go can be really persuasive. It's often quicker to reheat something than wait for a delivery, which is especially important at the end of a long day.

Some people like to batch prepare meals for the week ahead on a Sunday evening. This doesn't mean you have to prep every single thing you'll eat. Just make one or two large meals that you can divide up into daily portions. Curries, stews, and soups are perfect for this. You can make a giant batch and then store it until needed.

Changing your eating habits is a journey, it's not something that can be done overnight. They take time to develop, but once you've done this they'll be easy to stick with for the long-term. The key is to take positive steps every day. It's ok if you don't eat healthily at every single meal, just try to make healthier choices the majority of the time. In this way, you won't feel deprived (which is a sure-fire way to sabotage your efforts) and will be motivated by the progress you make.

Mindfulness vs Intuitive Eating

In addition to what you eat, the way you consume food is also important. Some strategies that have proven useful include mindful eating and intuitive eating. Although they sound similar they're actually quite different approaches. A good way to distinguish between the two is to think about when you can use them... Intuitive eating is something that happens BEFORE the meal whereas mindful eating happens DURING the meal.

Intuitive Eating

Intuitive eating is about tuning in to the signals that your body is sending out. We often eat out of habit because it's 'breakfast time' or we 'always eat after getting in from work'. This may not always be what our body needs, but the habits are so ingrained into our everyday life that we continue with them anyway.

Many people who are keen to avoid a 'diet mentality' will choose to adopt an intuitive eating approach instead. It encourages us to focus on hunger cues instead of the rules around what we 'should' or 'shouldn't' eat. A good way to pay attention to hunger cues is to think of hunger as a scale. Before deciding to eat, rate your level of hunger from 1 (extremely hungry) to 10 (too full). This can help you to identify what type of meal or snack you should prepare instead of doing so on auto-pilot. There are days when we feel hungrier and others where we want less, so this approach can help us tap into these cues.

This technique can also be applied during the meal too. When you've eaten around half of your plate, check in with your hunger and rate it on a scale or 1-10 again. If you feel satisfied (usually around a 6) then you could save the rest of your food for later or another day. Most of us will eat whatever is on our plate without any regard for how full we feel - this is something we think about only once we've finished. But by taking time to consider our hunger levels during the meal, we can avoid overconsuming calories when we don't really want or need them.

Mindful Eating

Mindful eating is about taking extra care to pay attention to our food as we eat it. Modern life is hectic with work and family commitments often leaving us feeling constantly busy. As a result, we often rush through the eating process because it's just another task that needs to be ticked off our to-do list. The problem with this approach is that it leaves us feeling less satisfied because we haven't really experienced the food as we eat it.

The mindful approach to eating encourages awareness and intention so that we slow down and truly experience the food. It involves making a concerted effort to notice the textures, flavours, and aroma of our meal so that we feel more satisfied at the end of it. Here are a few ways that you can incorporate mindful eating into mealtimes…

#1 - Pause

Before you dive into your meal, take a moment to pause and clear your head. Look at your food and slow your breathing. This will help to avoid eating on autopilot which is associated with unnecessary overconsumption.

#2 - Work Through Your 5 Senses

Tasting our food is the most basic way to appreciate it (although many of us eat too quickly to even manage this). Once we've slowed down, take a moment to consider the other aspects of your meal by working through your five senses. How does it look? What does it smell of? What textures can you feel? What sounds does it make as you cut or chew it? Try to isolate the different flavours within each mouthful and appreciate them individually.

#3 - Put Your Cutlery Down

Between each bite or mouthful, set down your cutlery. Only pick it back up once you've completely chewed and swallowed your food. Then you can start cutting your next piece or preparing the next mouthful. This can help to slow down the pace and avoid the mindless 'shovelling' that many of us do without thinking.

By combining intuitive and mindful eating into your mealtimes, you can transform your experience and start to heal your relationship with food. Pick one aspect to start with and incorporate it into your routine. Once you're doing it consistently and feel like you've mastered it, pick another one to add, until you're following all of the principles we've outlined.

ASK MY FUTURE SELF

Please complete the "ASK My Future Self worksheet" to slow down and think through your options when you encounter an impulse. Using a recent impulsive choice you made, answer the questions below to practice using this skill to reconsider what your options were in this situation. Find at least one opportunity to use this skill in the next week.

> **Attention:** Be aware of changes in your brain, body and behaviour.
> **Slow Down:** When you experience an impulse, pause and wait to do or say anything
> **Keep My Options Open:** List at least two choices you have in the moment.
> **My Future Self:** Consider how each choice will feel afterwards-is it likely to make you feel guilty?

Impulse I had was to:

What changes did you notice in your brain (thoughts), body (sensations), and behaviour when this impulse came up?

What was your reaction or response to the impulse (what did you do?) and how quickly did you make this choice?

Looking back on this situation, what options did you have about how to respond?

Imagining you could go back and talk yourself through this moment, what advice would you have given yourself to help make it easier to make the right choice?

STAYING ON TRACK

After you reach your goals, you will still need to pay attention to your eating habits. This way, if you notice any changes to your eating habits that are concerning, you can take action quickly to help you get back on track. It is normal that people who have struggled with overeating will need to be more aware and careful about their relationship with food, especially during times of stress. Use the spaces below to come up with a plan of what to look out for, and how to get back on track if you notice any changes.

CHANGES IN MY EATING PATTERNS WHICH MAY BE "RED FLAGS" FOR OVEREATING:

I.e.: eating out more, snacking at night	

THESE ARE THE STRATEGIES THAT I WILL CONTINUE BECAUSE THEY HELP ME STAY ON TRACK:

I.e.: food diary, meal planning, pack lunches	

BESIDES MAKING HEALTHY FOOD CHOICES, THESE ARE OTHER WAYS THAT I TAKE CARE OF MYSELF:

I.e.: eating out more, snacking at night	

STAYING ON TRACK CONTINUED

THESE ARE THE PEOPLE IN MY LIFE WHO ARE MOST SUPPORTIVE OF THE CHANGES I'M MAKING, AND WHAT I CAN COUNT ON THEM FOR:	
I.e.: my best friend, for support, to be an exercise partner	

THESE ARE THE WAYS (BESIDES MY WEIGHT) THAT I KEEP TRACK OF MY PROGRESS:	
I.e.: how my clothes feel, my energy levels	

WHEN I GET OFF TRACK, THESE ARE THE STEPS I WILL TAKE TO GET BACK ON TRACK:	
I.e.: make a meal plan, use a food diary, remove temptations from the pantry, etc.	

MY TOOLBOX

Use the space below to list some of the situations when you would be most likely to need your tools, and then work to add skills to your toolbox which might help in each situation.

Internal triggers (thoughts and feelings):

External triggers (situations, places, people):

What triggers feel like in my body (sensations) and sound like in my mind (thoughts):

The Tools in my Toolbox

HELPFUL THOUGHTS	HELPFUL SKILLS & STRATEGIES
HELPFUL ACTIVITIES	**HELPFUL PEOPLE**

Conclusion

At the beginning of this book, I shared that I wrote this guide to help you feel more in control of your eating habits.

I hope you now understand impulsivity and its role in the development and maintenance of binge eating behaviour. The journey forward is not "quick and easy" - but staying consistent and practising strategies that work for you is an important part of your recovery.

You have learned that it's important to work on how you think and act. This includes how you manage stress, your coping skills, addressing your inner critic and using compassion and self-care to improve your eating habits.

You should continue experimenting with sustainable and adaptive stress management, physical movement and nutrition. Pay attention to your psychological and emotional health by asking yourself:

- How do I regulate my emotions?
- What is working well for me?
- What other skills do I need to learn to improve how I feel and behave?
- Do I choose to ignore anything that might be damaging to my health?
- Am I kind and compassionate?
- What lessons can I take from my attempts to implement my latest plan to manage triggers?
- How can I implement the knowledge from this book to help me to succeed?

Finally, I want you to actively reject shame and other negative emotions. Instead, remember self-compassion. Being kind to yourself helps you form a healthier relationship with food sooner. Negative emotions and self-loathing only keep you from your goal, stuck in a pit of despair.

Your opinion and your health matters, so resist the pressure of becoming someone else's version of success. The more you apply your new knowledge of impulsivity and binge eating, the sooner you will feel more powerful and more in control of yourself and your behaviours.

This journey is one you can't escape. We all need to eat to nourish ourselves till the day we die. So, let's start this journey together. Remember, it's okay to experiment. You will stumble along the way. But, if you get back up, keep on taking small steps forward and apply the lessons you've learned here, you'll improve your relationship with yourself, and with food, and regain control.

Part 4 - Worksheets, Templates & Practical Activities

"Cultivate only the habits that you are willing should master you."
~ Elbert Hubbard ~

IMPULSE LOG

Use the log below to track each impulse you have to overeat and note how you responded. Use the last column to rate your response as either: positive (weakening the impulse), negative (strengthening the impulse), or neutral (no effect on the impulse). Use the examples below as a reference.

DATE	I HAD AN IMPULSE TO...	WHAT I DID IN RESPONSE	RATING MY RESPONSE
2/1/2019	Get a second doughnut	Got a second and third doughnut	☐ Positive ☐ Neutral ☑ Negative
2/5/2019	Get a soda from gas station	Bought a small can instead of 20 oz bottle	☑ Positive ☐ Neutral ☐ Negative
2/5/2019	Get a soda from gas station	Had an apple, threw the rest of the cake away	☐ Positive ☑ Neutral ☐ Negative
			☐ Positive ☐ Neutral ☐ Negative
			☐ Positive ☐ Neutral ☐ Negative
			☐ Positive ☐ Neutral ☐ Negative
			☐ Positive ☐ Neutral ☐ Negative
			☐ Positive ☐ Neutral ☐ Negative
			☐ Positive ☐ Neutral ☐ Negative
			☐ Positive ☐ Neutral ☐ Negative
			☐ Positive ☐ Neutral ☐ Negative
			☐ Positive ☐ Neutral ☐ Negative
			☐ Positive ☐ Neutral ☐ Negative

MODERATE EATING

When we are working towards making healthier eating decisions, moderation is a keyword that we need to keep in mind. Foods we commonly overeat (usually unhealthy foods high in calories and low in nutrients) are usually foods we need to think carefully about moderating.

Moderation includes both the amount of the food we eat, as well as how often we eat this type of food.

While in the early stages of changing our eating habits it may be necessary to cut out or restrict certain types of foods altogether, we often need to think about how to reincorporate these foods in moderate amounts later on. Use the worksheet below to plan how you will moderate some of your "trigger foods" that commonly lead to overeating:

Trigger Food	**Portion/Amount**	**How Often**
Example: potato chips	*1 small bag*	*2x / week or less*

MEASURING PROGRESS

While many people who are working to develop healthier eating habits describe a focus on weight, we need other ways to measure progress that do not focus on the scale. Besides the number on the scale, how else will you be able to tell you are making healthier food choices? Use the space below to brainstorm.

Area of Life	Specific Measure of Progress
Mental Health	*Example: not feeling guilty after eating*
Physical Health	*Example: feeling more energized throughout the day*
Social	*Example: being able to make healthy food choices with others*
Occupational	*Example: being able to say no to donuts at work meetings*
Recreational	*Example: being able to walk further without being winded*
Belief System	*Example: feeling more confident and in control of choices*

ENABLERS OR TRUE SUPPORTERS? CHOOSING THE RIGHT FRIENDS

IMPULSIVE OVEREATING ENABLERS or TRUE FRIENDS – CHOOSING THE RIGHT SUPPORTERS

It is hard to deal with temptations and urges, so don't make it harder for yourself. It might be easy to spot some of the people who will not be supportive of your plan to be healthy. The obvious ones might openly laugh at you and sabotage your attempts to become stronger in dealing with your impulsive overeating. Other people might be more subtle. They might just forget that you are trying to be healthy and come over with a chocolate cake. They might say that you don't always need to be good, 'So give yourself a break and eat some chocolate', or they might invite you to an open buffet for lunch. You need to pay attention to your support network and stay away from people who sabotage your success at the early stage when you are learning to change your behaviour. Right now, you need to surround yourself with cheerleaders for your progress! Be around people who encourage, motivate and support your goals/ you in your quest for change/self improvement. So who are your true supporters?

1. _____ 2. _____ 3. _____ 4. _____ 5. _____

Plan to succeed with people who truly care!

ADVANTAGES AND DISADVANTAGES OF IMPULSE BEHAVIOUR (UNHELPFUL IMPULSIVE BEHAVIOUR)

We can be creatures of habit, especially when it comes to impulsive actions. Even if it is not great for us or leads to negative consequences we often continue to behave impulsively because we feel that we have done so for such a long time. To help us to move past thinking this way and to establish a newer, healthier habit, we can do a cost-benefit analysis of our behaviour.

To start with, it is helpful if we look at our impulsive behaviour and ask ourselves the following questions:

What will be the benefits if you continue to behave this way? What does it give you?	What would be the disadvantages if you continue behaving impulsively? What will you miss about not following your impulses?
e.g. When I get I feel alive, I am excited, I want to win.	e.g. I am worried about my growing debt, I feel worthless, I am constantly lying to the people closest to me. I am scared to tell them, I feel like I let them down.
What are the disadvantages of stopping this behaviour?	**What are the advantages or benefits of stopping this behaviour?**
e.g. I will be so bored, what will I do then?	e.g. I will feel free, free of guilt and constant lies. I will be happy again, not having to hide all the time.

Take a moment to think about these questions as they relate to unhelpful impulsive behaviour:

Your example of unhelpful impulse behaviour is:
_____

What will be the benefits if you continue behaving Impulsively?
_____

What will be the disadvantages if you continue behaving impulsively?
_____
_____

What are the disadvantages of stopping with this behaviour?
_____
_____

What are the advantages/benefits of stopping it?
_____
_____

IDENTIFYING MY NEGATIVE THOUGHTS & COGNITIVE DISTORTIONS

We all have patterns of thinking that may impact the way we feel and behave. Often our thinking patterns are less than accurate. We all tend to think in extremes that don't fit with reality! Learning to recognise your own cognitive distortion will help you to ignore a negative thought or actively change it.

Recognising and changing your cognitive distortions will help you to change the way you feel and the way you behave. **Cognitive distortions are misperceptions and misinterpretations about what is really happening.** These misinterpretations are thoughts that come to our mind automatically.

How can you examine your negative automatic thoughts?

Try the following exercise:

Imagine you have an urge to do something quickly, without thinking about its consequences. Write your answers below:

Identifying my negative thought and cognitive distortions...		
Urge or Impulse to do:	**Negative thought:**	**Cognitive Distortion:**
"I have to have a glass of wine"	"It always happens to me. I never get what I want"	Overgeneralising

Situation #1
When I have an urge or impulse to do _____

My negative thought is _____

My negative distortion is _____

Situation #2
When I have an urge or impulse to do _____

My negative thought is _____

My negative distortion is _____

MODIFYING COGNITIVE DISTORTIONS/THINKING ERRORS

Awareness of your own 'cognitive distortions' or thinking errors means that you have a choice to change them, stay in control of your behaviour and decreasee any associated emotional discomfort and distress you experienced. In order to modify your thinking errors, consider the evidence for and against to determine for yourself whther engaging in impulsive behaviour is worthwhile. Follow the steps below to help you make the right decision.

Gratification

"I have to have sex now! If I feel this way I must have it now"

Evidence For:

- In the past it felt great to get what I want
- It feels cool not to care about anything and just go for it
- I like to get what I want

Evidence Against:

- Sex was really never that great
- I usually regret it as soon as I have finished
- I did not use protection, and panicked for days after about sexually transmitted infections

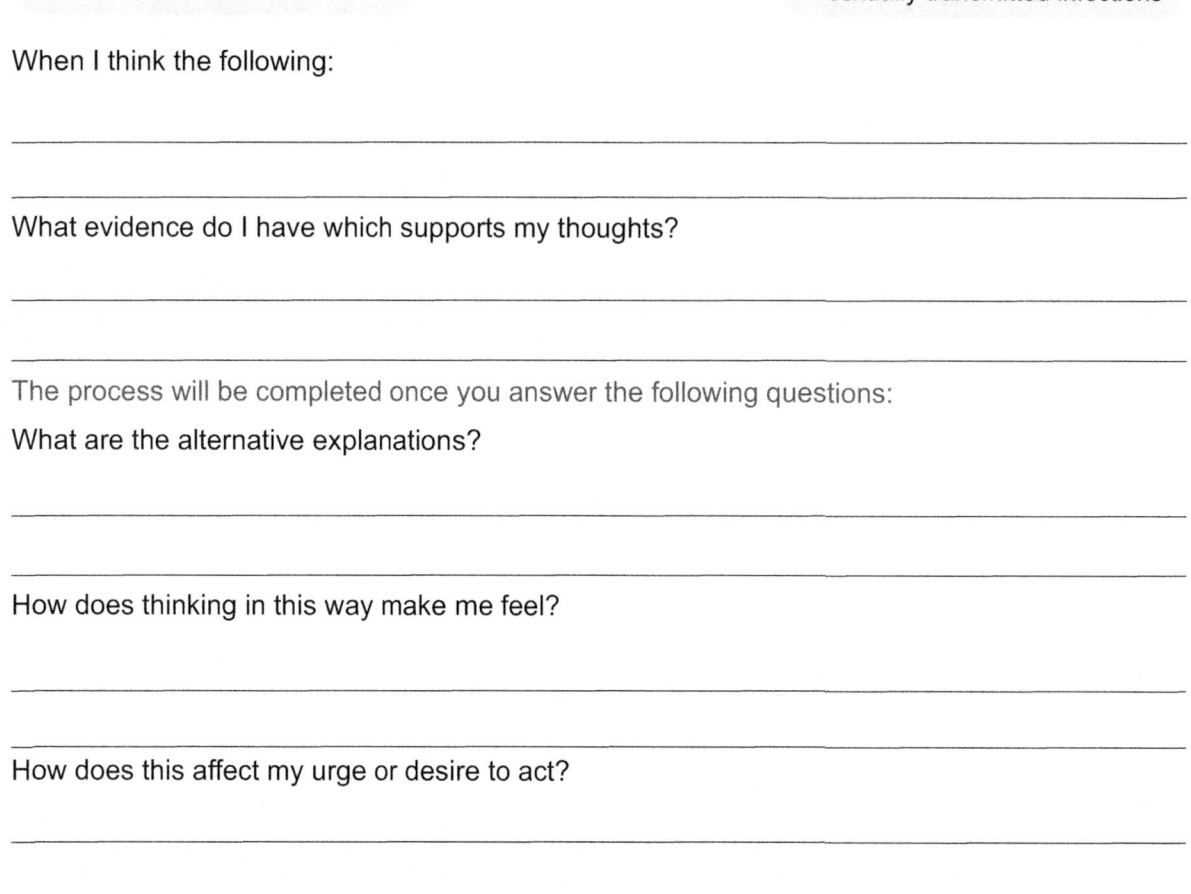

When I think the following:

_____

_____

What evidence do I have which supports my thoughts?

_____

_____

The process will be completed once you answer the following questions:

What are the alternative explanations?

_____

_____

How does thinking in this way make me feel?

_____

_____

How does this affect my urge or desire to act?

_____

_____

LIFE WHEN I AM IN CONTROL

If you have been behaving impulsively for a long time, the idea of trying to change such behaviour can seem daunting and difficult. At the same time, it is essential for you to identify and address such behaviours because they can be damaging and can impact on your quality of life.

Often we start focusing on all the problems and barriers and how difficult it would be for us to change such behaviour. Instead, you need to give yourself a chance to imagine a life when you are in control, when you can manage your emotions well, you know your triggers and can control your behaviours and your life.

Give yourself this chance. Right now, take a few moments and imagine your life to be different – imagine that you have already achieved your goal and you are in control. Let it be your first step. As the saying goes, if you can imagine it you can achieve it. Write down your list of improvements below, print it out and keep it on a pin board or somewhere where you can remind yourself that you can take control and improve your life.

Imagine on all levels what your life will be like when you stop this unhelpful impulsive behaviour.

If you have difficulties starting, use the following prompts.

If I not longer do _____

I will see the following improvements in these areas of my life:

My career
My friends
My close relationships
My financial situation
My hobbies/leisure
My feelings about myself
Some other positive changes will be...

....
....

Or

If I no longer behave/ do _____

My life will be better in so many different ways, such as:

_____
_____
_____

*"I am so looking forward to experiencing my life
when I am in control of my behaviour completely!"*

Notes

Notes

Notes

Notes

Notes

Notes

Notes

Notes

References

1. Ainslie, G. (1975). Specious reward: a behavioral theory of impulsiveness and impulse control. Psychological bulletin, 82(4), 463.
2. APA. (2013). Diagnostic and statistical manual of mental disorders (5th ed.). Arling- ton, VA: American Psychiatric Publishing.
3. APA. (2009). How technology changes everything (and nothing) in psy chology: 2008 annual report of the APA policy and planning board. Ameri can Psychologist, 64, 454- 463.
4. Arce, E., & Santisteban, C. (2006). Impulsividad: una revisión. Psicothe ma, 18(2), 213-220.
5. Arens, Z. G., & Rust, R. T. (2012). The duality of decisions and the case for impulsiveness metrics. Journal of the Academy of Marketing Science, 40(3), 468-479.
6. Arnow, B., Kenardy, J. & Agras, J. (1992). Binge Eating Among the Obese: a de- scriptive study. Journal of Behavior Med, Apr; 15(2): 155-170.
7. Arnow, B., Kenardy, J., & Agras, W. S. (1995). The Emotional Eating Scale: The de- velopment of a measure to assess coping with negative affect by eating. International Journal of Eating Disorders, 18(1), 79-90.
8. Back, S. E., Gentilin, S., & Brady, K. T. (2007). Cognitive-behavioral stress man- agement for individuals with substance use disorders: A pilot study. Journal of Ner- vous and Mental Disease, 195(8), 662-668. doi: http://dx.doi.org/10.1097/NMD. 0b013e31811f3ffd
9. Bergland, C. (2011, December 26). The Neuroscience of Perseverance. Retrieved from https://www.psychologytoday.com/ca/blog/the-athletes-way/201112/the-neuro- science-perseverance
10. Bernecker. (2014). Helping clients help themselves: Managing ethical concerns when offering guided self-help interventions in psychotherapy practice. Professional Psychology: Research and Practice, 45(2), 111.
11. Bickel, W. K., Odum, A. L., & Madden, G. J. (1999). Impulsivity and ciga rette smoking: delay discounting in current, never, and ex-smokers. Psychopharmacology, 146(4), 447-454. doi: 10.1007/PL00005490
12. Brunas-Wagstaff, J., Bergquist, A., Richardson, P., & Connor, A. (1995). The relationships between functional and dysfunctional impulsivity and the Eysenck personality questionnaire. Personality and Individual Differences, 18(5), 681-683. doi: http://dx.doi.org/10.1016/0191-8869%2894%2900 202-4
13. Caci, H., Nadalet, L., Bayle, F., Robert, P., & Boyer, P. (2003). Functional and dysfunctional impulsivity: Contribution to the construct validity. Acta Psychiatrica Scan- dinavica, 107(1), 34-40. doi: http://dx.doi.org/10.1034/j.1600-0447.2003.01464.x

14. Chamberlain, S. R., & Sahakian, B. J. (2007). The neuropsychiatry of impulsivity. Current Opinion in Psychiatry, 20(3), 255-261.
15. Cho, B.-H., Kim, S., Shin, D. I., Lee, J. H., Min Lee, S., Young Kim, I., & Kim, S. I. (2004). Neurofeedback training with virtual reality for inattention and impulsiveness. Cyberpsychology & Behavior, 7(5), 519-526.
16. Churchill, S., & Jessop, D. C. (2011). Too impulsive for implementation intentions? Evidence that impulsivity moderates the effectiveness of an implementation intention intervention. Psychology and Health, 26(5), 517-530.
17. Colbow, A. J. (2013). Looking to the future: Integrating telemental health therapy into psychologist training. Training and Education in Professional Psychology, 7(3), 155- 165. doi: http://dx.doi.org/10.1037/a0033454
18. Cyders, M. A., & Smith, G. T. (2008a). Emotion-based dispositions to rash action: Positive and negative urgency. Psychological Bulletin, 6, 807-828.
19. Delgado-Rico, E., Rio-Valle, J. S., Abein-Urios, N., Caracuel, A., Gonzalez-Jimenez, E., Piqueras, M. J., . . . Verdejo-Garcia, A. (2012). Effects of a multicomponent behavioral intervention on impulsivity and cognitive deficits in adolescents with excess weight. Behavioural Pharmacology, 23(5-6), 609-615. doi: http://dx.doi.org/10.1097/ FBP.0b013e 328356c3ac
20. Di Milia, L. (2013). A Revised Model of Dickman's Dysfunctional Impulsivity Scale. Journal of Individual Differences, 34(3), 138-142.
21. Dick, D. M., Smith, G., Olausson, P., Mitchell, S. H., Leeman, R. F., O'Malley, S. S., & Sher, K. (2010). Review: understanding the construct of impulsivity and its relationship to alcohol use disorders. Addiction biology, 15(2), 217-226.
22. Dickman, S. J. (1990). Functional and dysfunctional impulsivity: Personality and cognitive correlates. Journal of Personality and Social Psychology, 58(1), 95-102. doi: http://dx.doi.org/10.1037/0022-3514.58.1.95
23. Dobbs, R., et. Al. (2014). How the World Could Better Fight Obesity. McKinsey Global Institute Nov 2014.
24. Doll, S. (n.d.). Why Perseverance Is Your Secret To Success In Weight Loss. Retrieved from http://www.selfgrowth.com/articles/why-perseverance-is-your-secret-to- success-in-weight-loss
25. Farmer, R. F., & Golden, J. A. (2009). The Forms and Functions of Impulsive Actions: Implications for Behavioral Assessment and Therapy. International Journal of Behavioral Consultation and Therapy, 5(1), 12-30.
26. Forbush, K. T., Shaw, M., Graeber, M. A., Hovick, L., Meyer, V. J., Moser, D. J., . . . Black, D. W. (2008). Neuropsychological characteristics and personality traits in pathological gambling. CNS Spectrums,

13(4), 306-315.
27. Fox, K. (1997). Mirror Mirror: A summary of findings on body image. Social Issues Research Center. Retrieved from: https://www.sirc.org/publik/mirror.html.
28. Gagnon, J., Daelman, S., McDuff, P., & Kocka, A. (2013). UPPS Dimensions of Impulsivity. Journal of Individual Differences, 34(1), 48-55.
29. Garg, N., & Lerner, J. S. (2013). Sadness and consumption. Journal of Consumer Psychology, 23(1), 106-113. doi: http://dx.doi.org/10.1016/j.jcps.2012.05.009
30. Gay, P., Schmidt, R. E., & Van der Linden, M. (2011). Impulsivity and intrusive thoughts: Related manifestations of self-control difficulties? Cognitive Therapy and Research, 35(4), 293-303. doi: http://dx.doi.org/10.1007/s10608-010-9317-z
31. Grant, Donahue, & Odlaug. (2011). Overcoming Impulse Control Problems: A Cognitive- Behavioral Therapy Program, Workbook: Oxford University Press.
32. Grant, & Kim. (2003). Stop Me Because I Can't Stop Myself: Taking Control of Impulsive Behavior: McGraw-Hill.
33. Grant, J. E., Donahue, C. B., & Odlaug, B. L. (2011). Treating Impulse Control Disorders: A Cognitive-Behavioral Therapy Program, Therapist Guide: Oxford Universi- ty Press.
34. Green, L., Fisher, E., Perlow, S., & Sherman, L. (1981). Preference reversal and self control: Choice as a function of reward amount and delay. Behaviour Analysis Let- ters.
35. Harrington, N. (2007). Frustration intolerance as a multidimensional concept. Journal of Rational-Emotive & Cognitive-Behavior Therapy, 25(3), 191-211.
36. Heinlen, K. T., Welfel, E. R., Richmond, E. N., & O'Donnell, M. S. (2003). The na- ture, scope, and ethics of psychologists'e-therapy Web sites: What consumers find when surfing the Web. Psychotherapy: Theory, Research, Practice, Training, 40(1-2), 112.
37. Hodgins, D. C., & Peden, N. (2008). Cognitive-behavioral treatment for impulse control disorders. Revista Brasileira de Psiquiatria, 30, S31-S40.
38. Hollmann, M., Pleger, B., Villringer, A., & Horstmann, A. (2013). Brain imaging in the context of food perception and eating. Current opinion in lipidology, 24(1), 18-24.
39. Johnson, J. L., & Kim, L. M. (2011). The role of impulsivity in forgiveness. Individual Differences Research, 9(1), 12-21.
40. Joos, L., Goudriaan, A., Schmaal, L., De Witte, N., Van den Brink, W., Sabbe, B., & Dom, G. (2013). The relationship between impulsivity

and craving in alcohol dependent patients. Psychopharmacology, 226(2), 273-283.
41. Kaltenthaler, E., Parry, G., & Beverley, C. (2004). Computerized cognitive behaviour therapy: a systematic review. Behavioural and Cognitive Psychotherapy, 32(1), 31-55.
42. Kessler, R. C., Berglund, P. A., Chiu, W. T., Deitz, A. C., Hudson, J. I., Shahly, V., ... Xavier, M. (2013). The prevalence and correlates of binge eating disorder in the WHO World Mental Health Surveys. Biological Psychiatry, 73(9), 904–914. http:// doi.org/10.1016/j.biopsych.2012.11.020
43. Kim, S., Lewis, J. R., Baur, L. A., Macaskill, P., & Craig, J. C. (2017). Obesity and hypertension in Australian young people: Results from the Australian Health Survey 2011–2012. Internal Medicine Journal, 47(2), 162-169.
44. Lally, P., Van Jaarsveld, C. H. M., Potts, W. W., & J. Wardle. (2009). How Habits are Formed: Modelling habit formation in the real world. Europan Journal of Social Psy- chology, 40(6), 998-1009.
45. Leehr, E. J., Krohmer, K., Schag, K., Dresler, T., Zipfel, S., & Giel, K. E. (2015). Emotion regulation model in binge eating disorder and obesity-a systematic review. Neuroscience & Biobehavioral Reviews, 49, 125-134.
46. Loeber, R., Menting, B., Lynam, D. R., Moffitt, T. E., Stouthamer-Loeber, M., Stallings, R., . . . Pardini, D. (2012). Findings from the Pittsburgh Youth Study: cogni- tive impulsivity and intelligence as predictors of the age-crime curve. Journal of the American Academy of Child & Adolescent Psychiatry, 51(11), 1136-1149. doi: http:// dx.doi.org/10.1016/j.jaac.2012.08.019
47. Logue, A. W. (1998). Laboratory Research on Self-Control: Applications to Administration. Review of General Psychology, 2(2), 221-238.
48. Lyke, J. A., & Spinella, M. (2004). Associations among aspects of impulsivity and eating factors in a nonclinical sample. International Journal of Eating Disorders, 36(2), 229-233.
49. Macht M. (1999). Characteristics of eating in anger, fear, sadness and joy. Appetite 33, 129–139 10.1006/appe.1999.0236
50. Meule, A. (2013). Impulsivity and overeating: a closer look at the sub scales of the Barratt Impulsiveness Scale. Frontiers in psychology, 4.
51. Mobini, S., Grant, A., Kass, A. E., & Yeomans, M. R. (2007). Relationships between functional and dysfunctional impulsivity, delay discounting and cognitive distortions. Personality and Individual Differences, 43(6), 1517-1528. doi: http://dx.doi.org/ 10.1016/j.paid.2007.04.009
52. Mobini, S., Pearce, M., Grant, A., Mills, J., & Yeomans, M. R. (2006). The relation- ship between cognitive distortions, impulsivity, and sensation seeking in a non-clini- cal population sample. Personality and Individual

Differences, 40(6), 1153-1163. doi: http://dx.doi.org/10.1016/j.paid.2005.11.006

53. Moeller, Barratt, Dougherty, Schmitz, & Swann. (2001). Psychiatric as pects of im- pulsivity. The American Journal of Psychiatry, 158(11), 1783-1793. doi: http://dx.-doi.org/10.1176/appi.ajp.158.11.1783

54. Moeller, & Dougherty. (2002). Impulsivity and substance abuse: What is the connec- tion? Addictive Disorders & Their Treatment, 1(1), 3-10. doi: http://dx.doi.org/ 10.1097/00132576-200205000-00002

55. Neff, K. D. & Dahm, K. A. Self Compassion: What it is, what it does, and how it re- lates to mindfulness. Link: http://self-compassion.org/wp-content/uploads/publica- tions/Mindfulness_and_SC_chapter_in_press.pdf

56. Parry, C. J., & Lindsay, W. R. (2003). Impulsiveness as a factor in sexual offending by people with mild intellectual disability. Journal of intellectual disability research, 47(6), 483-487.

57. Peters, J. R., Erisman, S. M., Upton, B. T., Baer, R. A., & Roemer, L. (2011). A pre- liminary investigation of the relationships between dispositional mindfulness and im- pulsivity. Mindfulness, 2(4), 228-235. doi: http://dx.doi.org/10.1007/ s12671-011-0065-2

58. Pitts, S. R., & Leventhal, A. M. (2012). Associations of functional and dysfunctional impulsivity to smoking characteristics. Journal of Ad diction Medicine, 6(3), 226-232. doi: http://dx.doi.org/10.1097/ADM.0b013e31825e2a67

59. Racine, S. E., Keel, P. K., Burt, S. A., Sisk, C. L., Neale, M., Boker, S., & Klump, K. L. (2013). Exploring the relationship between negative urgency and dysregulated eating: Etiologic associations and the role of negative affect. Journal of abnormal psychology, 122(2), 433.

60. Raji, C. A., Ho, A. J., Parikshak, N. N., Becker, J. T., Lopez, O. L., Kuller, L. H., ... & Thompson, P. M. (2010). Brain structure and obesity. Human brain mapping, 31(3), 353-364.

61. Romer, D. (2010). Adolescent risk taking, impulsivity, and brain develop ment: impli- cations for prevention. Developmental Psychobiology, 52(3), 263-276.

62. Rusting, C. L. (1998). Personality, Mood, and Cognitive Processing of Emotional Information: Three Conceptual Frameworks. Psychologi cal Bulletin, 124(2), 165-196.

63. Sarah Fischer, Kristen G. Anderson, and Gregory T. Smith University of Kentucky. Coping With Distress by Eating or Drinking: Role of Trait Urgency and Expectancies 2004

64. Schmidt, R. E., Gay, P., Ghisletta, P., & Van der Linden, M. (2010). Linking

impulsivi- ty to dysfunctional thought control and insomnia: a structural equation model. Jour- nal of sleep research, 19(1‐Part‐I), 3-11.

65. Sharma, Markon, & Clark. (2013). Toward a Theory of Distinct Types of "Impulsive" Behaviors: A Meta-Analysis of Self-Report and Behavioral Measures. Psychological Bulletin.

66. Sharma, Sivakumaran, & Marshall. (2011). Deliberate self-indulgence versus invol- untary loss of self-control: toward a robust cross-cultural consumer impulsiveness scale. Journal of International Consumer Marketing, 23(3-4), 229-245.

67. Sharma, L., Kohl, K., Morgan, T. A., & Clark, L. A. (2013). "Impulsivity": Relations between self-report and behavior. Journal of Personality and Social Psychology, 104(3), 559-575. doi: http://dx.doi.org/10.1037/a0031181

68. Silverman, W. H. (2013). The Future of Psychotherapy: One Editor's Perspective. Spinella, M. (2004). Neurobehavioral correlates of impulsivity: Evidence of prefrontal involvement. International Journal of Neuroscience, 114(1), 95-104. doi:http://dx.- doi.org/10.1080/00207450490249347

69. Smyth, J.M., Wonderlich, S.A., Heron, K.E., Sliwinski, M.J., Crosby, R.D., Mitchell, J.E., & Engel, S.G. (2007). Daily and momentary mood and stress are associated with binge eating and vomiting in bulimia nervosa patients in the natural environ- ment. Journal of Consulting and Clinical Psychology, 75, 629-638.

70. Stanford, M. S., Mathias, C. W., Dougherty, D. M., Lake, S. L., Anderson, N. E., & Patton, J. H. (2009). Fifty years of the Barratt Impulsiveness Scale: An update and review. Personality and Individual Differences, 47(5), 385-395.

71. Stratton, K. J. (2006). Mindfulness-Based Approaches to Impulsive Behaviors. New School Psychology Bulletin, 4(2), 49-71.Stroebe, W., van Koningsbruggen, G. M., Papies, E. K., & Aarts, H. (2013). Why most dieters fail but some succeed: A goal conflict model of eating behavior. Psychological review, 120(1), 110.

72. Suris, A. M., Lind, L. M., Kashner, M. T., Bernstein, I. H., Young, K., & Worchel, J. (2005). Aggression and impulsivity instruments: An examination in veterans. Military Psychology, 17(4), 283-297. doi: http://dx.doi.org/10.1207/s15327876mp1704_3

73. Sutin, A. R., Ferrucci, L., Zonderman, A. B., & Terracciano, A. (2011). Personality and obesity across the adult life span. Journal of Personality and Social Psychology, 101(3), 579.

74. Tobin, H., & Logue, A. W. (1994). Self-Control Across Species (Colum

75. Ulla Kärkkäinen, Linda Mustelin, Anu Raevuori, Jaakko Kaprio, Anna Keski-Rahko-nen: Successful weight maintainers among young adults—A ten-year prospective population study. Eating Behaviors. 7th March, 2018 online. DOI 10.1016/j.eatbeh. 2018.03.004
76. Walcott, C. M., Marett, K., & Hessel, A. B. (2014). Effectiveness of a computer-assisted intervention for young children with attention and reading problems. Journal of Applied School Psychology, 30(2), 83-106. doi: http://dx.doi.org/ 10.1080/15377903.2013.874389
77. Wang, L. P., Li, F., Wang, D., Xie, K., Wang, D., Shen, X., & Tsien, J. Z. (2011). NMDA receptors in dopaminergic neurons are crucial for habit learning. Neuron, 72(6), 1055-1066.
78. Weissman, A. N., & Beck, A. T. (1978). Development and validation of the Dysfunc- tional Attitude Scale: A preliminary investigation.
79. Weller, Cook, Avsar, & Cox. (2008). Obese women show greater delay discounting than healthy-weight women. Appetite, 51(3), 563-569.
80. Whiteside, S. P., & Lynam, D. R. (2001). The five factor model and impulsivity: Using a structural model of personality to understand impulsivity. Personality and Individual Differences, 30(4), 669-689.
81. Wiecha, J. L., Hall, G., Gannett, E., & Roth, B. (2012). Development of healthy eating and physical activity quality standards for out-of-school time programs. Childhood Obesity (Formerly Obesity and Weight Man agement), 8(6), 572-576.
82. Wiers, R. W., & Stacy, A. W. (2006). Implicit cognition and addiction. Current Directions in Psychological Science, 15(6), 292-296.
83. Winkel, D. E., Wyland, R. L., Shaffer, M. A., & Clason, P. (2011). A new perspective on psychological resources: Unanticipated consequences of impulsivity and emotional intelligence. Journal of Occupational and Organization al Psychology, 84(1), 78-94.
84. Wittmann, M., & Paulus, M. P. (2008). Decision making, impulsivity and time perception. Trends in Cognitive Sciences, 12(1), 7-12.
101. World Health Organization. Obesity and overweight fact sheet. (2018, February 16). Retrieved from http://www.who.int/news-room/fact-sheets/detail/obesity-and-over- weight
85. Zilberman, M. L., Tavares, H., & el-Guebaly, N. (2003). Relationship between craving and personality in treatment-seeking women with substance-related disorders. BMC Psychiatry, 3, 1. doi: http://dx.doi.org/10.1186/1471-244X-3-1

Impulsivity Courses

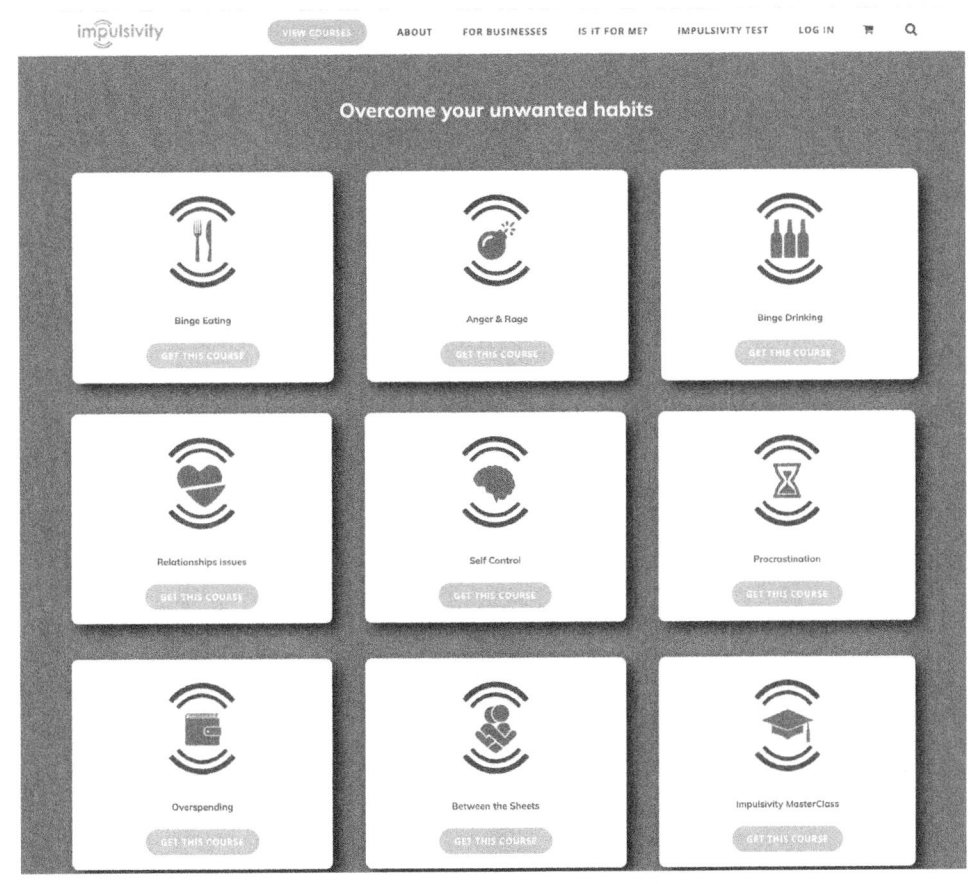

Go to https://impulsivity.com.au/ to learn more.

Our program "Beat the Binge" provides you with all the resources you need to achieve the change you are seeking for:

- 15+ video lessons that walk you through various powerful CBT techniques and mindfulness strategies
- Practical activities that allow you to put what you're learning into practice
- Printable easy-to-follow worksheets for you to complete
- A library of mindfulness exercises and guided meditation recordings
- Lifetime access to all of the course content and future updates
- Certificate of completion
- Visit https://impulsivity.com.au/ to learn more about our comprehensive online program.

About the Author

Beat the Binge

Yuliya Richard
PsyD Health and Clinical Psychology

Dr Yuliya Richard is a Sydney-based clinical psychologist working in private practice. For almost 20 years she's helped people battle addiction, overcome emotional distress, change their unhealthy habits and improve their relationships.

After researching dysfunctional impulsivity as part of her Doctoral Thesis, Dr Richard founded the Impulsivity Online Project in 2015. A web-based program, Impulsivity is an innovative approach to recognising, managing and overcoming impulsive behaviours. Helping clients manage their urges as well as those whose trust has been damaged by repeated impulsive behaviours, Impulsivity features courses focusing on binge drinking, anger management, binge eating, overspending, procrastination and more.

An accessible, affordable and effective way for people to regain control of their lives, Impulsivity is a great first step and/or complementary tool in overcoming impulsive behaviours. Find out more at https://www.impulsivity.com.au.

Printed in Great Britain
by Amazon